Simply Leadership

Bite sized guidance for practical leaders

Malcolm Maclean

Simply Leadership

Bite sized guidance for practical leaders

Malcolm Maclean

© 2017 - 2019 Malcolm Maclean

Also By Malcolm Maclean

D3 Tips and Tricks v3.x

Leaflet Tips and Tricks

Raspberry Pi: Measure, Record, Explore.

Just Enough Linux

Just Enough Co-Authoring in Leanpub

Just Enough ownCloud on a Raspberry Pi

Just Enough Raspberry Pi

Just Enough Ghost on a Raspberry Pi

Just Enough Nagios on a Raspberry Pi

D3 Tips and Tricks v4.x

Never Enough Ice Cream

Raspberry Pi Computing: Temperature Measurement

Raspberry Pi Computing: Ultrasonic Distance Measurement

Raspberry Pi Computing: Analog Measurement

PiMetric: Monitoring using a Raspberry Pi

For the Team

Contents

Introduction	1
Welcome!	1
Who is this book for?	2
Simply Leadership	3
Qualities	5
Authenticity	6
Clarity	11
Approachability	15
Empathy	17
Empowerment	20
Nurturing	27
Supportive	32
Personable	36
Professionalism	38
Inclusive	44
Appreciative	48
Knowledge	51
Innovation	52
Delegation	56
Communication	58
Strategy	62
Being Open Minded	67
Experience	73

CONTENTS

Practicality	80
Observation	89
Curiosity	95

Attitude **97**
Calmness	98
Be Inspiring	102
Motivation	110
Restlessness	113
Collaborative	115
Self Awareness	117
Positivity	124
Assuredness	127
Disciplined	129
Aspire	132

Approach **135**
Persistence	136
Resilience	138
Passion	140
Focus	142
Decisiveness	146
Commitment	155
Patience	158
Consistency	161
Courage	162
Confidence	172
Realism	177
Flexibility	180
Progressive	182

Values **185**
Honesty	186
Acting Ethically	189
Trustworthiness	192
Transparency	194

Accountability	195
Responsibility	199
Respect	207
Humility	212
Generosity	215
Selflessness	217

Introduction

Welcome!

Hi there. Congratulations on being interested enough in leadership to have gotten your hands on this book.

Hopefully this will be an entertaining and informative journey that will help you think about how you approach leadership and how you can be more effective in your role. I know that this sort of book has been written by others, but I have an ulterior motive. I write books to learn and reflect on what I'm doing. The hope is that by sharing the journey perhaps others can learn something from my efforts :-).

Ambitious? Perhaps :-). But I'd like to think that if you're reading this, I managed to make some headway. I dare say that like other books I have written (or are in the process of writing) it will remain a work in progress. They are living documents, open to feedback, comment, expansion, change and improvement. Please feel free to provide your thoughts on ways that I can improve things. Your input would be much appreciated.

You will find that I have a pretty rough language style. I should have studied harder in English at school. My only hope is that any teachers I had during that time have long since retired and won't have the inclination to delve into leadership roles.

There's a **lot** of information in the book. There's a vast amount of 'propositions', some of which people will no doubt take issue with. Sorry about that. I've scraped up these by taking notes and remembering snippets of information from experience gathered over many years. Some will be based on quotes from historical or notable figures. Foolishly I never kept any references for these and I suspect that where they might be appropriate I will have butchered their words so that any errors are entirely mine.

I'm sure most authors try to be as accessible as possible. I'd like to do the same, but be warned... There's a good chance that if you ask me a technical question I may not know the answer. So please be gentle with your emails :-).

Email: d3noobmail+leadership@gmail.com

The image used on the cover is part of the painting of Nikola Šubić Zrinski's charge from the fortress of Szigetvár by Johann Peter Krafft, 1885[1].

Who is this book for?

You!

Just by virtue of taking an interest and getting hold of a copy of this book you have demonstrated a desire to learn and to improve. That's the most important criteria you will want to have when trying to develop yourself. Your experience level will come second place to a desire to learn.

---

[1] https://en.wikipedia.org/wiki/Siege_of_Szigetv%C3%A1r

Simply Leadership

Leadership is the process of guiding a team to follow a plan. It embodies responsibilities on many levels to ensure that the mission is achieved, that the businesses plan is followed and that individuals are cared for. It demands a great deal from those who accept a leadership role and in many ways it is its own reward.

The hierarchy of what we will examine is broken down into characteristics, traits and propositions.

The characteristics of leadership that we will examine are;

- The personal qualities that a leader should have
- The aspects of leadership that should be known or learned.
- The attitude that an effective leader should adopt.
- The approach a leader should take dealing with their responsibilities.
- The values that a leader must display.

Qualities

The 'Quality' characteristic is a reflection of the personal qualities that are demonstrated in a leadership role.

This characteristic perhaps more than the others highlights the distinction between *managing* a team and *leading* a team. Traits such as authenticity, clarity and empathy, while being approachable and personable, have a very 'touchy-feely' sound to them, but a leader has to *care* about their team to be effective.

You will need to understand that your team is a machine that needs to have constant maintenance to be reliable. For it to be a thing of elegance, form and function, you will need to be involved in all aspects of its care and upkeep, so that it can perform to a high standard.

The qualities that we will examine are;

- Authenticity
- Clarity
- Approachability
- Empathy
- Empowering
- Nurturing
- Supportive
- Personable
- Professionalism
- Inclusion
- Appreciation

Authenticity

Authenticity is the property of being a 'real' person and having the experience to be able to inspire respect for your character.

Leaders need to be able to demonstrate that they are competent and capable. This is most effectively done by practical example. A leader that can 'walk the walk' will foster respect and trust from their team.

You will always be at an advantage in a leadership role if you have had experience carrying out some of the more foundational work that your team does. Having gotten your hands dirty in the past gives you kudos for 'knowing the business' and demonstrates that you're not in a leadership position by accident. You will have a pedigree by which you can be measured. Hopefully your time working as one of the general team was positive and can be used to your advantage. If you come into a leadership role without any experience in the actual work, look for opportunities to learn something specific to help give you context and to show that you take a genuine interest. Seek out those members of your team who have good corporate knowledge and experience and get a feel for the organization from them.

Occasionally get your hands dirty.

A leader should be able to demonstrate mastery of a practical skill to reinforce that they have capability to do things that keep them in touch with the 'real world'.

There is a two pronged reason for retaining a practical element in your working life. Firstly being able to reinforce that you have skills that extend beyond your leadership role adds to your credibility. It's not showing off, but more a confirmation that you aren't in the position by accident. Your team will be able to relate to a practical skill slightly easier than the leadership requirements and this will help them have confidence in you. Secondly, you should keep your practical skills tuned as they should act as a catalyst for keeping you engaged and content. In the same way that your team members should feel a sense of pride in doing a good job, you should feel good about your competence in the practical world.

Maintain a slight air of mystery. You shouldn't be an open book.

A leader should embody the positive aspects of the organization they work for and be a role model for their team. Aspects of themselves which are not common knowledge should enhance their reputation.

This advice might sound slightly nonsensical, but you should keep some of yourself *to* yourself. You need to be someone that your team looks up to, but knowing everything about you dilutes how they regard you. You will have war stories and anecdotes to pass on, but be very wary of repetition. Your personal details lose relevance unless they are business related. In areas outside work a slight air of mystery helps reinforce a humble / modest character as well as demonstrating that you have a personal space that you would wish to maintain to yourself. If practical, having a specialist interest or skill that is only ever obliquely referenced is a way of demonstrating expertise and leaving a possibility of more.

Understand who you are and what matters to you. Then let the team know.

Each individual has a leadership style that is particular to themselves and each wants to apply that style in a way that is a reflection of who they are and how they want their team to operate. These aspects of leadership should be reflected on and articulated to the team.

You have a way of working that is unique. Everyone does. Sorry, you're *not* special in that regard. But you have a responsibility to make sure that your team knows what is expected of them and how your vision of an effective workplace will operate. Take time to reflect and plan how you want to achieve your team's goals. This will include the type of approach that your team will take such as focusing on productivity, profits, customers or growth. Will you have the flexibility to train and develop staff or do you need to push your business to achieve critical objectives. What degree of communications do you expect and how will the business plan be developed. These are all parameters that will drive your expectations and actions. Being able to articulate how the team should proceed will help everyone work more cohesively.

Tell war stories. They will inspire and provide a sense of history. Beware of repetition.

Experience passed on via word of mouth is a good way to include the team in the history of the business and to illustrate interesting aspects how the organization has developed. There is potential for these anecdotes to be colorful tales which will be interesting on first hearing, but will decline in effectiveness with repetition.

Recounting stories is a natural aspect of a workplace and one that can be used to develop and build a culture. These can include cautionary tales where the story illustrates examples of where things went wrong, exemplars of heroic efforts that overcame significant odds or humorous anecdotes that entertain but probably ultimately fall into the "learning from failure" or "notable effort" categories. Whatever the case, be careful not to disparage others unnecessarily, even for the sake of humor, and use the opportunity to have the story provide an example of expectations for the team. For example, a failure that demonstrates strength of character, an incident that identified a way to improve safety or selfless actions that helped a customer. These tales are an essential part of an organization's history, but be aware of your audience so that you avoid boring them with repeated stories.

Leadership is not determined by technique but by traits of character.

Effective leadership will be the result of a natural expression of personal characteristics. Regurgitation of lessons will be sufficient to provide guidance, but a leader *is* a leader. They don't have to have to consider *how* to act, the way that they behave is natural and instinctive.

Some leaders find that their actions have always been effective at guiding a team and getting the best from their work. Others who aren't lucky enough to be naturals at the process use lessons and experience to reinforce appropriate behaviours, so that they become second nature. Leaders in this position shouldn't regard their efforts as any less effective, it's just the approach that requires modification. The adage "fake it till you make it" provides a good example of how this method works. The longer you can use learned techniques to provide effective leadership, the more natural your responses to the role will become. Employing this mechanism is, by itself, recognition of your determination to be successful in your work.

The person you honor will indicate the kind of person you are.

Respect is an indicator of intent. Emulation of characteristics signals a desire to improve and develop a in a positive way. Strong role models provide opportunities for growth.

Those that we regard as heroes are the people that strongly influence how we want to develop. Find good role models and be one yourself. Take time to discover people who represent ideals that you value. Learn about them and how they maintained their way in the world. Take heed of their influences and make them your own. Immersing yourself in the positive influences of others will have a natural effect of guiding your own actions and character. In that same vein you must realize that you will also be held up as a role model for others. Act accordingly, with the knowledge that your influence will extend beyond the immediate advice you give.

Clarity

Clarity is the property of communicating in a way such that confusion about what is said is minimized.

A leader needs to be able to communicate clearly and concisely. Clarity removes doubt about what is being communicated and being concise is efficient. This encompasses all form of communication and is independent of the audience.

Clarity in the way that you communicate can be considered in two ways. Clarity of message and clarity of intent. Clarity of message describes the semantics of delivering information. Practise and hone the skills required to speak clearly to a group or an individual. Use good grammar and express yourself in a way that minimises the number of words required without losing the intent. Clarity of intent is ensuring that you accurately convey what you *mean*. Complex topics can find themselves mired in convoluted but accurate language. Take care to understand your audience and couch your communication methods appropriately.

Give orders that make sense.

Instructions need to be given that are clear, unambiguous and logical.

Giving direction does not require highly detailed explanation or explicit instructions. You can tailor your orders to your team on a case by case basis depending on the task and the person carrying out the activity. However, what you ask people to do needs to make sense. Not just to you, but to the person that is receiving the instruction. Think carefully about the context of the information as well as the intended audience. If, after you have directed an action, you notice that the activity doesn't quite gel with your expectations, just check in to establish if everything is proceeding as both parties intended. Always give the recipient of an order the opportunity to ask for clarification. Either at the time it is given or at any point where they might require more information.

Don't be afraid to use imperative verbs.

Direct instruction helps remove ambiguity. A leader is expected to be a source of direction. Giving orders is part of a leadership role. When either swift action or emphasis is required, an imperative verb will help.

There *can* be a general reluctance to give orders. It might be a feeling that you aren't being polite or that there should be greater autonomy given to your team. Leadership requires that you have a good relationship with your team and that they understand your requirements. Imperative verbs emphasize haste and reinforce the narrow focus of this type of direction. Don't make orders your default setting for giving instructions. Your team needs to be able to use their initiative. It also helps you provide an extra degree of emphasis when you *do* use imperative verbs.

A statement should not sound like a question.

Framing a request or a statement as a question creates confusion and opportunity for misinterpretation.

This type of occurrence can happen for a couple of general reasons. The first is where the speaker is unsure of the statement and wants some form of confirmation. The second is when the technique is used in a form to belittle the receiver. Neither of these instances is acceptable from a leader. They're self-demeaning and create situations where there is confusion and doubt. When you are on the receiving end of this type of event be up front and ask for clarification. Often the speaker will be unaware of what they are doing.

Avoid euphemisms. Clarity begets honesty.

Avoid any artificial construct that detracts from the clarity of your message.

It is always tempting to use metaphors and euphemisms when communicating. Whenever possible, use clear, plain English explanations. This advice is not opposing different methods of getting ideas across. An analogy or metaphor is a useful tool when necessary. But this would only be the case when a simple explanation has failed. The more that the message deviates from the original format, the greater the opportunity for misinterpretation. As with all abstraction, avoid it whenever possible.

Be unambiguous and authoritative when responding to questions.

A leader should pride themselves on being able to respond to a question in such a way that the questioner can be satisfied with the answer or they will be in possession of the next step to *find* the answer.

Answering questions should be bread and butter for leaders. Whenever you're asked a question it's a validation of the role that you have. Consider it appropriately so that you carry out due diligence. If you don't know the answer, look for the best way to find the information required. Never speculate on an answer without providing a caveat. Provide references if necessary. Always respond clearly. Don't dance around the topic. If your audience is interested in some history of why you answered as you did, provide it. Remember, you should always be aiming for your team to be able to determine their own answers, so where appropriate take people through the process.

Approachability

Being approachable is the quality of making people feel comfortable about bringing you information.

A leader lives and dies by the information that they can gather and process. You need to ensure that your team is happy to come to you for any reason. They are an extension of yourself and form a vital role in keeping you accurately informed.

You can't suddenly decide to be approachable. It's a perception issue that people will have about you and therefore it will take time to develop the reputation required for people to to trust you. Often it can be difficult to ensure that the quality of information reaching you is right. You will need to build your approachability by sacrificing some degree of relevance in the first instance till you can 'train' your team to make sure that the right level of detail is delivered. You will know that you have succeeded when they come to you with things that they have done wrong.

If your team is afraid to talk to you, they may not give you the information you need.

A leader needs to ensure that they are available to their team and that more importantly the team needs to know that they will always be listened to.

Your team are your eyes and ears. They are an extension of your senses and as such you need to ensure that they are able to provide you with the information that you need to operate effectively. Don't be afraid to interrupt other business to talk to a team member. Even if it's to get the gist of the issue so that you can get back to them later. Always pay attention to what is being said and stay alert for any subtext as you may find that your team members are hesitant about raising sensitive topics. Treat all conversations with seriousness and pay attention. Make notes if necessary and if you are taking an action to do something, make sure that you get back to them to let them know of the outcome. If some team members are being a bit over cautious and bringing things to you that *they* can deal with, don't be afraid to empower them to help you out.

Empathy

Empathy is the quality of caring for the needs of others.

A leader needs to be able to identify with the support requirements of their team and customers, so that they can help them and better understand their needs. Empathy assists both parties in forming a supportive relationship.

Empathy is an interesting human feature. It's more of an emotional response than a teachable trait. That doesn't mean that you can't be empathetic, but if it's not your natural response you are going to have to work on it. Caring for others is valuable because ultimately at some point we all need help. If your team members observe you caring about others, then they should make the logical leap to assuming that you will care about them. This in turn engenders good will and trust. Both of which are positive factors in promoting engagement and job satisfaction. A good rule of thumb is to pretend that you're their mother. A little fussing over your team (without getting weird) can be positive.

Empathy is not a weakness

The ability to relate to your team members means understanding and sharing their feelings. Engagement is promoted by a common perspective and caring about what the wider organisation does. Empathy is the key enabler to drive understanding and engagement.

A traditional view of leadership has a stoic figure showing no emotion as they organise their resources with detachment. The thought being that displaying emotions or appearing to care about your team members would be viewed as a weakness. More modern thinking tells us that a leader needs to have a better understanding of their team members and in particular they need to be able to relate to them on a personal basis. This action breeds an environment where individuals feel supported and protected and where in turn they provide reciprocal support. Achieving this goal may not necessarily come easily to all. It takes time and effort to develop an effective empathic skill set since everyone is different. Pay attention to your team members and how they behave to each other. Listen (*really* listen) and reflect what you hear emotionally. As an example if a team member is concerned, you should demonstrate that you understand that they're concerned. Give a voice to what you see and hear. Take every opportunity you can to form a bond of trust that demonstrating empathy allows. Caring about your team will lead to them caring about you.

Small acts of kindness show you care and demonstrate character.

Being able to demonstrate that you care about your team helps them gain confidence in you and the wider team. It can be done in small ways that reinforce your reputation and promotes engagement.

Often when people think of attributes that define character they are drawn to the 'big ticket' items like courage and fortitude. Opportunities to demonstrate these are limited, but it is possible to maintain a constant reminder in your team of your degree of care for them and by extension your character, through simple acts of kindness, to engender positive feelings about the workplace. It should be stressed that this isn't some mechanism to artificially manipulate how people feel about themselves or their work. This should be a normal practice that recognises effort and promotes engagement. It's easy to forget that in spite of people getting paid to work, the vast majority choose to do so for a particular organisation because they want to feel valued and in turn to provide value. To help this you can do the little things that reflect their commitment. For example, say thank you, remember birthdays, listen without interrupting, compliment where appropriate to someone's boss, bring in morning tea, smile, clean up the coffee area or buy a raffle ticket from colleague's children's fund-raiser.

Keep an eye on your team members and ask if everything's okay if you see a negative change.

As a leader you need to maintain awareness of your team member's state of mind. If you see something that is out of character, you need to be able to approach them to assist if possible or to just be supportive if appropriate.

One of the main reasons for staying engaged with your team is to ensure that you can pick up on subtle indicators of when things might not be going well. These can often manifest as changes in behaviour or approach that will be subtle and will require attention. Just as important as *noticing* when something has changed, is having the courage and compassion to check in with them to determine if there is something you can do to help. Often this is as simple as asking *"Is everything okay?"*. If you haven't done it before, it might sound a little touchy-feely or intrusive, but often it will be the catalyst that will allow someone with a problem to be able to come forward and seek assistance. You need to ensure that this happens sooner rather than later, since problems that go on for too long have a tendency to develop into larger issues that may require more effort in resolving. Be sensitive to others needs for privacy, but don't be afraid to make yourself available. Even if everything is fine, the person will remember that you cared enough to ask and this may encourage them to seek assistance if trouble strikes in the future.

Empowerment

To empower someone is to provide them with the authority and the means to control their own destiny.

A leader should always be looking for an opportunity to delegate actions to their team. This enables diversification of knowledge, demonstrates trust and aids in personal development. At the same time it promotes engagement by giving team members more autonomy to carry out their work.

In the parlance of encouraging engagement of your team, any opportunity to promote autonomy, mastery and purpose is going to be a good thing. Empowering your team to do things that help them control the way they work is a significant enabler that has both short and long term benefits. In the first instance you will be removing some of the work that you are currently doing (assuming that it can be safely done by others) and in the longer term, those empowered have the opportunity to do work that helps them grow their skill-set and gives them greater ownership of the business. This in turn should improve personal confidence and corporate resilience. Be careful to make sure that you *really* do let go when you take these actions, but at the same time keep a weather eye on how things are going and make yourself available to provide advice or guidance.

Empower others to lead when you are unable to.

A leader's primary responsibility is to the business and its mission. Any hierarchy should have a default succession plan prepared and understood.

Your role is to lead your team to support the mission. You won't always be available and you won't be there forever, so your team needs to be able to carry on in your absence. The best way to do this is to ensure that you have delegates trained and prepared to provide support when required. Always look for opportunities for others to step into roles of responsibility. The more familiarity your offsiders have carrying out the role, the easier it will be to ensure that the functions of the team continue uninterrupted. The two main activities that you can promote are making training available and providing opportunities for gaining experience. Spread the responsibility for acting in your place so that there is more than one person available to step up if required. This will help your delegates have a good support structure in place.

If a team member needs to become more responsible, give them more responsibility.

Professional and personal development require a balance of training and experience. Responsibility is effectively developed by placing individuals in positions where they can put the skills into practice.

Your team's growth needs to be a continual process. There will be the natural progression of building skills and experience, but improving responsibility requires a slightly different approach. Because accepting responsibility is more of a "values based" activity, you need to use exposure to situations that provide learning experiences to drive development. Accepting responsibility and being responsible means making decisions based on selfless altruistic principles. A person needs to be able to reflect and internalise their own needs compared to the needs of their wider environment to then make decisions that support their task. The more this can be practised the better they will get. An important part of the process is the use of mentoring to provide guidance and feedback. Taken in isolation it is very difficult to decide if what a person is doing is the right thing, but a separate point of view allows for more objectivity.

Good team members love what they do. Back off and let them enjoy their work.

Enjoying work is a strong indicator for engagement and productivity. Where this is self driven and providing a positive business outcome, any intervention should be minimal.

Staff enjoying their work and contributing to business outcomes is the best result that any leader could want. The best advice when you find yourself in this position is to avoid disturbing it. Be aware that there can be a tendency for leaders to want to meddle in situations where things are going well. Some will find that they want to be associated with a positive aspect of the business in such a way that they can better understand it. Some will want that success to be associated with themselves (you don't want to be that person). Accept that good things can happen without your intervention. Don't meddle where you can just stand back and admire things going well. Rest assured, happy employees and teams are a positive reflection on their leaders, irrespective of how they come about.

Give your experts time to think for themselves. It will encourage creativity.

A team will contain subject matter experts that are capable of advanced thinking in their areas of strength. Maximizing this capability requires that they be allocated time to research and explore options.

Providing opportunities for your team to innovate is a great way to improve engagement and business processes. Everyone wants to be able to do things well. Your experts have that capability, but in order to do awesome things they need time. That time is required because getting from the known to the unknown requires considering things in new ways. This doesn't happen without an opportunity to explore advanced topics in an environment that promotes thinking deeply. A lack of interruption is widely regarded as beneficial since the process of context switching from one train of thought to another interrupts concentration. So give them good periods of contiguous time for best results.

Every team member should have control of something they understand.

Providing opportunities for responsibility and mastery improves engagement and helps maintain systems in a proactive way.

Giving people opportunities to become experts in something has a tangible benefit to the business. The individual will enjoy the experience because they have influence in their own destiny and to an extent in the business. The feeling of having control is a powerful motivator and one that can improve people's enjoyment of what they do. At the same time they will be becoming an expert in the area that they control. This provides the business with enhanced corporate knowledge and opens opportunities for development and greater efficiency. The team member can also associate their efforts with the business in a more tangible way which gives them ownership and "buy-in" to the organization in general.

Be comfortable laughing at yourself, but never at your co workers.

A relaxed attitude to self depreciation is healthy and demonstrates comfort with personal strengths and weaknesses. A leader should never assume that any member of their team will be as comfortable.

Being able to laugh at yourself is a good thing. It demonstrates that you have good self-awareness and are in touch with the real world in the sense that you recognize a situation that is funny for its own sake. It's always infinity better for you to be laughing *with* the rest of the team at something you did than them laughing *at* you while you're not there. It also shows that you are emotionally mature and resilient. This should be something that your team should use as an example for personal development if required. It is **not** suitable for you to make fun of your team members. You can laugh *with* them, but never *at* them. Certainly don't initiate a humorous story at someone's expense and if one is initiated in your presence without them there, you need to be careful about how you respond. If a joke is being made about them at their expense you are approving of it unless you demonstrate otherwise. Jokes in poor taste or denigrating of others should be treated as unacceptable.

Don't be afraid to take occasional time out. Your team can handle things fine without you.

Taking a break is an important part of staying healthy and maintaining a good work-life balance. There should be a suitable support hierarchy in place to manage a leader's temporary absence.

You need to keep yourself healthy and maintain that condition. Everyone imagines themselves as fit and healthy until they aren't. The takeaway message is that looking after yourself needs to be a proactive thing where you carry out preventative maintenance on a regular basis. Empower your team so that there is a good alternative command structure that allows all members to know how to carry on in the absence of any of the team. This obviously takes pre-planning and concurrence from those who would step into new roles and at the same time you need to ensure that leading up to your absence, you bring your deputy up to speed with any ongoing activities.

To grow leadership in your team, send them on jobs without you.

Leadership development needs to be an ongoing process. Those who would assume the responsibility require training and experience to prepare them for the role.

You should be actively growing and developing leadership skills in your team. The more responsibility that they can assume the greater the flexibility of the team in general. Enabling this requires people who are suitable and willing to step up and appropriate preparation. The preparation should be a combination of training and experience in the specifics of a leadership role. This will mean that you need to actively provide opportunities for them. Now comes the tricky part. In the ideal world someone gaining experience can have a mentor close by to guide them and provide something of a safety net should they have problems or questions. While this is possible for leadership roles, there is no substitute for being on your own and having to work things out yourself. Ultimately to grow good leaders, they need to be prepared, encouraged and then released to do the job.

Give your team a goal and let them figure out how to achieve it.

An effective team is a one that can function as a cohesive, autonomous unit. They should be able to draw on the strengths inherent in the team to achieve their goals. Even when the pathway to success is unknown, they should be able to use their strengths to more forward and complete their tasks.

Your team is comprised of different people. They should be aware of the relative strengths of each other and of the expertise that each can bring to bear in completing their tasks. Your role is to make sure that they have the knowledge and confidence to be able to do the jobs required of them. Success breeds success. Any chance that you have to encourage your team to get on with work independently with a minimum of guidance from you, is a great achievement. Give them opportunities to explore what they can do and to test their capabilities. This will enable them to grow in confidence and ability. You need to make sure that they have the environment that they need to enable this to happen.

Pick good people to do what you need done, and let them get on and do it.

Successful teams are built on recruiting and training the right people. The business needs will drive the skill-set and the character of the team will enable a successful approach. Once in place the team should be capable of operating mainly independently.

Recruiting is one of your most important responsibilities. It takes time and care to identify the appropriate skills and knowledge required to meet the business needs. Selecting capable team members is a combination of matching that need to skills and ensuring that the personality of the individuals will fit into the team dynamic. Take your time. Do it right. Everyone is different and will have their strengths and weaknesses, but look for the right character and values to drive a successful recruitment. Don't compromise on either of these. You may be tempted by external pressures to recruit to a specific number or to drive a particular task. To do so is short term thinking that will cause problems in the long term. With the right people in place, nurture the skills required and you should be able to set them a problem and just step back.

Nurturing

To nurture is to care for and protect others while encouraging their development.

Nurturing your team is the way by which a leader ensures that there is a strong culture of support that promotes personal and professional development in the group.

Helping your team to become better personally and professionally is one of the cornerstones of good leadership. Part of that effort comes from directly involving yourself in helping and guiding others. This should be part of a broader range of 'soft skills' that you should employ to make sure that your team feel valued and encouraged to grow. To do this you need to take a very personal interest in individuals and to make sure that their needs are met and that their individual goals can be realised. It is very much **your** responsibility to make sure that you team develop positively.

Once basic needs are taken care of, team members will focus on the purpose of their work.

Complex tasks require people to be able to concentrate. Removing concerns about simple things allows easier focus on the hard things.

People are employed to carry out work of varying degrees of difficulty. The more complicated the task, the more specialised the expertise to carry it out. Being able to clear your mind and concentrate allows greater focus and will ultimately achieve better results. The aim of an employer and a leader is to remove distractions wherever possible and as a result, improve work output. This will typically require an up-front investment and you will have to use your judgement to determine the best returns. For example, if your staff are normally employed at a desk using a computer, then it would make sense to provide them with a large enough screen to see all the work they need to do at once with a responsive mouse and an easy to use keyboard. They should be in a chair that is comfortable to use for long periods and in an environment that doesn't leave them too hot or cold. If they need to rely on external processes to carry out their role, these should be as hassle free as possible to avoid the disruption caused by context switching. You will never be able to keep everyone perfectly happy, but wherever practical, take steps to remove potential barriers to people being able to focus on their tasks.

After a period of pressure, ensure that the team and yourself have ample recovery time.

When you and your team have been working particularly hard, you need to provide an opportunity for all concerned to relax and recover.

Working under pressure is a good thing in that it promotes extending your capabilities and generally improving the team's ability to work in difficult conditions. But this is only sustainable for a limited time. Constantly working under pressure will burn people out and will create an environment of stress and difficulty. Make sure that you recognise when the team have been operating under these conditions and when they have finished you need to make sure that there is an opportunity to rest and recover. This doesn't have to be everyone taking leave or throwing a large party. Just make sure that there is the ability to recover from the pressures by avoiding them adequately for a time. If you have an opportunity to celebrate achieving a hard fought for goal this should be taken, but mostly look for a chance to relax a bit and recharge the batteries.

Watch over your team. They're your responsibility.

You should think of your team like you think of your family. Make sure you look after them and they will look after you.

Fundamentally you should care about your team. It shouldn't just be a job, you should *want* to do it. Each member of the team should understand their role and responsibilities. They should be able to get on with their work secure in the knowledge that you will be taking care of them. You are accepting a significant responsibility by acting in a leadership position and that responsibility acts in two ways. You look after the team so that they can concentrate on their jobs and your organisation needs you to make sure that your team functions smoothly so that they can achieve their assigned goals. Once both of those things happen your job is done.

Promote engagement by giving the most interesting work to other team members, not yourself.

Encouraging your team to enjoy and value their work comes down to making sure that they have opportunities to work on tasks that will encourage them to feel positive about what they are doing. Your job is making sure that they work effectively.

This advice should be self-evident and if you find yourself hoarding interesting work you need to correct that immediately. Not only would it be a selfish act, but it will have a directly detrimental effect on your team as they could rightly presume that you care more about your own needs than the teams. In areas where you have an interest and expertise you need to ensure that you get others trained and experienced so that you can pass on the responsibility. In doing so it should be obvious that you are wanting to improve other's enjoyment and this will indirectly improve engagement.

Guiding others to success is at the heart of leadership.

A leader's role is to guide a team to successfully complete assigned tasks. That success breeds confidence and enthusiasm. Any team that can approach their work with both of those attributes immediately has a head start to a positive outcome.

It should be noted from the outset that your job is to ensure that your team members can achieve their goals. Always resist the urge to do something yourself when you could empower a member of the team to do it instead. Giving people ownership of the problem and the solution will naturally lead to a feeling of accomplishment when they succeed. Repeated successful outcomes becomes self-perpetuating.

Your satisfaction will come from others success.

The process of ensuring that your team feel positive about their work helps them achieve success. You should derive your own sense of accomplishment and pride in your work when this happens.

People will find satisfaction in different ways in their work. As a leader your accomplishments are as a direct result of the achievements of your team. You should feel pride in their work and their successes. It's important that you have a good mechanism for enjoying your role. Take opportunities to celebrate and reflect on the positive effect that your team has had. Always remember that when your team has succeeded you have succeeded.

Attract, nurture, coach, and retain talent.

Improving your team should be a continuous process that provides opportunities for development, advancement and personal growth.

Your team should be seen as a place that people want to go to, where opportunities for development are available and the skills of the members are relevant and in demand. The process of improving the expertise in your team starts with identifying what the required skills are and what sort of person can provide that resource. It will always be difficult to grow experience without a base to build on. Look for experience initially when building capability. Once it has been established look for smart people. They don't necessarily need to have all the skills you need straight away but they should have a strong desire to learn. Use your internal resources to encourage personal development and support. This will promote collaboration and retention. There will always be some turnover in staff. These should be opportunities for celebrating their contribution and identifying what the new balance of skills are.

Supportive

Being supportive is the act of providing encouragement or help to others.

Providing support to a team ensures that they feel confident about carrying out their assigned tasks safe in the knowledge that if there is something that needs to be addressed outside of their immediate control they have options.

Supporting your team can take many forms. This can range from the simply helpful acts of assistance to encouraging people's development to reassuring team members in their decision making processes or even sympathising with them when things don't go according to plan. Providing support helps build trust and gives your team confidence in going about their jobs. It doesn't hurt to be overt about making sure that they know you are there for them and when asked you **need** to make sure that you carry through on your obligations.

> **If your team know their jobs, leave them alone. If they don't, help them learn.**

A leader is a guide. Micromanaging a team is not necessary when they are working in their area of expertise. When direction is required a leader will be able to put their team onto the right path.

I have never met anyone who has claimed that they enjoy being micromanaged. Learn to recognise that supporting your team is not an excuse for intruding on their work. They are professionals who are competent at what they do. You have succeeded when you can stand back and tasks get completed without any input from you at all. The one area where you will need to provide guidance is when their knowledge set is not wide enough. Reinforce with the team that asking for guidance is more than acceptable, it is part of a culture of success. Learning from others and in turn passing on expertise is a sign of a high-functioning group. Take any opportunity to encourage and promote this. In the meantime, when your team is getting on with their work, leave them alone.

When a team member's behavior changes significantly, inquire and investigate.

Altered behaviour is typically prompted by some form of event or change in a person's life. A leader can support the individuals in their team by ensuring that factors that impact on them personally are addressed appropriately or taken into account.

We all go through significant events during our lifetimes. These can vary on a spectrum from things such as poor health, bereavement, relationship milestones such as marriage and divorce, birth of a child or even spiritual changes. For better or for worse, they happen. As a leader you need to be alert to changes in behaviour that will be an indicator of an event that could be affecting your staff. If it is negatively impacting them, they could require guidance or some form of support. Often just knowing that assistance is available can be a valuable aide. Don't be shy about enquiring. It's your job. Be discrete and sensitive. Don't be pushy. If the change is impacting on the individual's performance in their job, make them aware so that you can both work to solve the problem.

When team members are unsuccessful, encourage them to try again.

Success is a combination of effort and goal attainment. The effort has merit in and of itself and even if the goal hasn't been achieved, there will be lessons learned. Team members can take those lessons and try again with foreknowledge. The key is having the encouragement and the support to persevere.

Your team will have ups and downs. Failure is never pleasant, but we all need to accept that it does happen. Not succeeding in a particular venture is a moment that knocks confidence and is a natural inhibitor to continuing. When members of your team are in a down cycle following not achieving their goals, encourage them to review and learn. Armed with that new knowledge they will be in a better position to look at possibilities for future success. This is the point where you can provide positive support to reinforce that you have faith in them and their abilities. The review is always necessary to determine if the goal actually *is* attainable, but that should be discoverable with an honest appraisal. Document the lessons learned and plan the next approach. Whatever you do, don't let the same mistakes be repeated and continue learning.

Defend your team members.

A leader has responsibility for all aspects of their team. Any adverse comments or actions taken against them needs to be addressed.

Your team won't always get it right. You will find yourself in the position of responding to criticism at some point. Whether right or wrong you need to address any and all concerns. That's obviously not intended to mean that you defend poor behaviour or substandard work, but it does mean that you front up to any concerns on your team's behalf. They are an extension of your will. If things haven't gone as planned, front foot any criticism so that you own the problem **and** the solution. Others can criticise *you* but they shouldn't be attacking your team. If there are any disciplinary issues to work through or corrective action to be taken, then *you* will do it.

Take your experts at their word, however surprising their assertions may sound.

Subject matter experts have a depth of knowledge on topics which will lead to observations and insights that would ordinarily be difficult to make. As a result, their discoveries can be unusual or counter-intuitive. Whatever the case, respect their opinions and act accordingly.

A leader should have a broad overview of all the areas that they have responsibility for. Your team will be the experts in the various areas that make up the sum total of your sphere of influence. That expertise will manifest itself in a range of different ways. Occasionally those will surprise you. Irrespective of the degree of surprise involved, take their advice seriously. Specialising in a subject required dedication and a degree of sacrifice (as they don't get as many opportunities to diversify), so recognise that their opinion is the result of a process that is designed to make insightful analysis of situations which others simply couldn't reproduce. That skill and experience is your resource. Trust it. Don't miss an opportunity to get clarification so that you understand the impact and external effects of what they are saying, but recognise the expertise for what it is.

Personable

Being personable is the characteristic of being pleasant and easy to get along with.

A leader should try to be as personable as possible. This will assist in being approachable and make it easier for your team to be able to communicate honestly with you. It also helps in maintaining relationships with all stakeholders.

Being personable is not a 'must have' for a leader, but for those who are, it is a useful tool in making a more effective team. Becoming more approachable and likeable in general helps put others at ease and encourages the wider group that you need to interact with, to communicate with you openly. There will be times when you need to be more direct, but these should be circumstance driven and less of a default setting. Always aim to get along with others. Engage in social occasions and ensure that when people leave your company they take a positive impression with them.

It's okay to be kind.

A leader needs to be able to demonstrate 'people' skills to direct, motivate and inspire. These traits are not incompatible with being kind to those around them.

Your role as a leader means needing to stand slightly apart from your team. This is in order to avoid a degree of 'over-familiarity' that could affect your ability to make decisions that are in the best interests of the mission. It also prevents any perception of a conflict of interest or favouritism with individuals. In spite of this you need to have a genuine empathy with your team members and you need to be able to take into account their personal hopes and dreams. In relating to your team (and in general) you should always make the effort to be generous and considerate. Your team will look to you for moral guidance and examples of acceptable behaviour. Any opportunity you have to demonstrate the standard that you want others to adopt should be taken. This doesn't mean being taken advantage of or having your time monopolised, but it does mean paying attention to your team at a personal level, genuinely caring about their welfare and acting appropriately on that.

Keep meetings short. Take your time when talking with individuals.

Meetings can have a tendency to consume more time than they are due. Always look to ensure that they are managed efficiently. However, individuals need to be looked after in a more considerate way. One on one conversations should not be rushed and wherever possible result in a positive outcome.

There is much made of the tendency for meetings to be inefficient and to eat into time by going off topic or being coerced into agendas that aren't planned. If you're running a meeting you need to be ruthless in ensuring that they stay on topic and meet the needs that have been laid down for them. Keep an agenda and publish minutes. Ensure that actions are recorded and that they are reviewed for completion. Actively seek to gain a reputation for no-nonsense meetings. This style of personal interaction should be in contrast to any one on one sessions that you have with your team members. Always allow time for topics that they care about and maintain a sympathetic ear for any concerns that they have. You need to be approachable and to be someone that can get things done to help people at a personal level. Even if it's passing on advice or sympathising at an unfortunate situation. Listen and respond in a way that helps them.

Professionalism

Being professional is the action of being reliable in doing your job well.

A leader needs to maintain a professional approach so that they are regarded as an authority in their line of work. This in turn gives others confidence in their abilities so that in times of need they can seek your advice or rely on your competence.

Being professional is as much about your behaviour as it is about the way you do your work. It means you should project confidence in your abilities and that you should be regarded as a reliable person. There are a range of small things that will enhance this. Be on time, communicate appropriately, meet your deadlines or negotiate new ones early, keep your word, be friendly, dress and act in a dignified way. You will recognise that these are good general points of advice, but when coupled to a leadership role it promotes confidence in you, your team and the work you do. Always aim to do a good job. Set standards that are high so that people can identify you and your team with quality. Hone your skills to become an expert and share the secrets of your success with others, thereby forming better relationships and promoting your skill-set.

Be professional, and take pleasure in your work. Both are possible.

A leader should always be an embodiment of professionalism. In itself this should be a pleasurable objective and one that enables a sense of satisfaction. But overall they should choose work that engages them and which they naturally enjoy.

As a leader you should work hard to achieve your goals and to ensure that your team is functioning well. Those around you should see an engaged individual that takes an obvious pride in doing their job well. This needs to be a genuine aspect of your working life. No amount of faking it will make you enjoy a job that you dislike. The achievements of your team reflect on you. Enjoy that feeling. Feed it back into ensuring that the standards that you set maintain and enhance your working life and the environment of those around you. Take time to reflect on and appreciate the work that you do. While a leader will always strive to improve, recognise that achieving a high standard is a positive outcome that you can take pride in. Allow yourself to enjoy the feeling of having accomplished something good.

Be the coach for your team, not their parent, or their drill sergeant.

A leader needs to be able to guide their team to success. Orders and direction are only effective in certain situations.

You need to have a relationship with your team that isn't based on authority. Work *with* them to achieve goals. Help them to become engaged in the organization's success. A team that gets used to just doing what it's told will *only* do what it's told. Your team should be excited to take the initiative in tasks and in doing so will achieve things that you will never have thought of. They will only get to this point by ensuring that they understand that the **team** dynamic will be their key to success. Instil this by encouraging independent thought. Promote communication and collaboration in all activities. In other words *coach* them to achieve **any** task. Don't *tell* them how to achieve **one** task.

The World is a ridiculous place. Maintain your dignity.

With so many people in the World, there is what appears to be infinite opportunities for participating in something that could be viewed as absurd. Maintaining a sense of balance and leading by example is important for a leader.

Many people are familiar with having taken part in a "*What was I thinking?*" moment. As a leader you are setting the tone for those around you. Your actions have consequences that affect how others behave. Think carefully about what you get involved with, lest it reflect poorly on you and influences your team adversely. We should caveat this advice by saying that there is a difference between 'eccentric' or 'unusual' and 'ridiculous'. You *can* have a pastime that others would find odd. That's fine. The problem comes about when people view what you do as crossing a line into the realm of 'weird' and 'undignified'. There is no actual line that shall not be crossed. You will need to use your judgement to decide what does and doesn't qualify as unacceptable. When in doubt seek advice from someone you trust (a partner or similar).

A tidy appearance reassures your team and instantly provides a positive first impression for others.

A professional appearance is an indicator to any outside observer that a person *cares* about making a positive impression.

Maintaining a tidy appearance takes a little effort. By itself that's a reason why not everyone will do it. Use the method of dressing appropriately to tell those around you that you went to an effort to appear respectable. Perhaps you didn't *need* to, but you chose to do so because you have a preference for maintaining a standard. It is possibly easier to flip the statement somewhat to observe that *anyone* can dress scruffily. The person who is dressing down *could* be an outstanding leader who is, well organised and has everything in control, but if faced with only the image of someone with a tidy appearance and someone who is scruffy, the preference will always go the the person who has made the effort. It's human nature. We can say *"Don't judge a book by it's cover"* as much as we like. The truth of the matter is that we do and your team will feel reassured by their boss having a professional appearance.

If you have mannerisms, ensure that they're socially acceptable.

Habits or foibles that others would find unsettling are not traits that are acceptable for an effective leader. They will cause doubts and concerns in their team and others, that will make them difficult to support.

In the ideal world the leader of a team will be a symbol that will inspire respect and be a role model. To achieve this you need to be able to minimise any outward signs that might be interpreted as deviating from acceptable norms. These aren't things that are obviously wrong or illegal, they are actions or behaviours that aren't appropriate for the role. For example, the use of offensive profanity or not bathing often enough, would be upsetting to many people and by extension, when they think of you, their thoughts are coloured with the belief that you have concerning character flaws. Where these flaws exist, other problems could exist with your ability to lead. If you have an issue, hopefully you can identify it and take steps to change positively.

Everyone makes choices, but ultimately our choices make us.

Every action that a person makes helps define who they are and the byproduct of those choices is the reinforcing effect on the individual.

We all make choices throughout our lives. They are a natural part of day to day activity. A leader is required to make a lot of decisions that have an impact in their professional role. Those professional choices are intended to decide on a direction or between different options. Our personal choices determine how we behave and develop. A leader needs to be able to think about how to improve themselves constantly and then implement changes in their lifestyle that make those improvements operative. Decide to become a better person through reflection and personal development. Look at ways that your weaknesses can be mitigated or improved. Decide to change your habits to improve yourself physically or mentally.

Every time you speak, you need to demonstrate the characteristics of leadership.

A leader is a symbol for their team and their organisation. When they communicate they need to embody the characteristics of a leader so that the message is received and automatically associated with the intended outcome.

A leader shouldn't speak unnecessarily. Don't be frivolous with your words or talk just for the sake of hearing your own voice. You need to be able to communicate succinctly and with authority. When you speak, your team needs to feel reassured that you are in control of the situation and that you know what you're doing. Using slang words or expletives does not convey the impression of a professional. Use techniques and mannerisms that help express your ideas without becoming a caricature. In the same way that your appearance and actions should convince people that you are acting professionally, your choice of language and delivery needs to leave no doubt that the speaker of the words understands what they're talking about and should be listened to.

You're going to meet some idiots and infidels. Be the better person.

A leader need to be able to rise above those around them to provide a strong, stable model of acceptable behaviour. This is the influencer that will assist others and set the tone for all interactions with the team.

Time and experience will allow you to meet a wide range of individuals. There is a tendency for people to exist in something of a bubble where the the people that they interact with are similar to themselves. At the same time we can often dismiss what we see on television news as things happening in a different world or associate it with entertainment / fiction. The sad fact of the matter is that there is a wide range of personality types and abilities. Not all of them will be motivated to make the World a better place and some will have a very distinct 'self interest above all else' mentality. Some will be people that, while well meaning, will struggle with complex topics (but may not realise it). In short you need to realise that the spectrum of abilities and motivations is wide. Don't allow a lower standard for behaviour influence how you act. You need to be the example that will elevate others.

Inclusive

Being inclusive is about ensuring that there is a range of different experiences and points of view in your team.

As a leader you need to be able to drive for a homogeneous representation of people on your team so that you are able to benefit from the range of life experiences that will better support the way you do business. The drivers (amongst others) are improved problem solving, higher creativity and greater flexibility.

People experience many different aspects of life, from different educations, genders and cultural backgrounds. It's important to ensure that you maintain a balance of experiences in your team so that it can recognise different needs and accurately deliver useful services to customers. This will mean identifying shortfalls in representation and avoiding the generation of barriers that would prevent diversity. Always promote a broad reach to problem solving that actively supports drawing from a broad pool of knowledge. Encourage thinking from alternative viewpoints and draw different ideas into general consideration.

Your team should feel welcome and appreciated. There are other groups they could move to.

You should always treat your team members with common courtesy and respect. Always remember that they *choose* to work for you. They could just as easily choose to work for someone else.

Being polite costs nothing but it gains you a happy workplace. Happy personnel are far more likely to be productive and engaged in their work. Always remember that all things considered we will spend a significant portion of our waking hours in the company of the people that we work with. You want that environment to be a positive one. The little things are important. Say "hello" in the morning like you mean it. Remember things about your staff that you can bring up in conversation to show them that you care about them and their welfare personally. Let them know when they've done well. Thank them at the end of the day. Look out for their personal needs and take action if things don't look right. Support them honestly in your dealings with others. Remember that you don't have to be their friend, but you want them to know that you value them.

If your deputy has a different way of doing things, make sure you both agree on the outcomes.

You and your right hand person will naturally have different ways of getting the job done. Remember that it's okay to approach things differently, but it's vital that you are working towards a common goal.

It's important to have a second in command so that your team have a reference point for guidance if you're not there. The position of deputy doesn't have to be permanent. It could be rotated to expose different team members to responsibility or personal development. It could also be a set role that has a trusted lieutenant to back you up. Whatever the case, you need to accept that they will have a different way of doing things to you. Different doesn't mean bad or wrong, there is always more than one way to go about a task. However, irrespective of the way that a body of work is carried out you need to ensure that the both of you have agreement on the goal that you are working towards.

Create an atmosphere of trust, not fear.

When people work in an area where they feel supported and valued they will be more productive and engaged. If they feel concerned or fearful they will not work to their full potential.

A work area that has an atmosphere of trust is one where people feel free to work hard without fear of negative ramifications if things go wrong. Trust is as much about the support from the environment as it is the personal support from the leader of a group. That's why it's important that as a leader you create a place to work that will foster innovation and responsibility. The entire group need to be self supporting. If the reverse is true you will have personnel that will refuse to take risks that could improve the way they do work and the environment will be one of recrimination and intolerance.

Be patient with team members' idiosyncrasies. Everyone is different.

Realise that everyone will act, react and interact with their surroundings and others in different ways. This is normal and something to be valued in a diverse team.

Diversity in a team is about having a range of different skills and viewpoints that can be applied to a problem to achieve a successful outcome. The good news is that diversity comes naturally by virtue of the fact that everyone is different. Of course that sounds incredibly predictable, but what you will need to accept as a leader is that it is the diversity of a functional team that will help it succeed. The worst situation you could find yourself in would be where you are trying to solve a problem and you were working in a group where everyone thought the same way and had much the same experiences. This means that everyone will have a degree of feeling as if everyone else is 'different'. So long as 'different' isn't something that works against the functioning of the team this is a positive.

Encouraging competition between team members is the opposite of your job.

The aim of a team is to have a group of individuals working collaboratively to achieve a goal. A competition is a naturally divisive activity that does not promote overall togetherness.

Human beings are a naturally competitive species. We shouldn't imagine that this is a bad thing. It promotes drive and enthusiasm to excel. However, when applied to team members it works directly against the principles of team building. For starters, a competition has two entities trying to achieve the same goal separately. This is an incredible waste of resources. That's before we start digging into the human dynamics of the idea. In a competition there is a winner and one or more losers. In a competition between team members the aim is not to win *for* your team, it's to win *against* your team. Let's not play that game.

Brainstorm alternative solutions with your team to gain fresh ideas and commitment.

To maximise the opportunity for innovation and get a team supporting a project, involve them in the process of working out the best solutions to problems.

Being part of a team means **feeling** like part of a team. Having your opinion considered by your peers and having an opportunity to influence decision making is a sign of respect. From a group perspective, having a wide range of perspectives to draw on provides opportunities to leverage diverse thinking. It's a win for both sides and one that helps a team maintain a healthy balance. The other bonus is that people involved in developing a solution to a problem will naturally be supporters of the outcome.

Appreciative

Being appreciative is about recognising other's efforts and acknowledging them positively.

Team members feel valued when they are rewarded for their efforts. Appreciation is a mechanism for ensuring that your team are aware that you value them *and* their skills. This promotes feelings of satisfaction and encourages them to seek positive reinforcement again through good work.

Appreciating the work of your team can be the simplest thing in the world. Just saying "thank-you" is one of the most powerful drivers to increased feelings of satisfaction that can be employed and its cost is nothing. When milestones are achieved or goals met, make sure that you recognise the effort that went into the work and the achievement itself. Don't overdo the gratitude or pass it on when it's not warranted. This will devalue more deserving work. Try to make the appreciation personal. Your team should associate you with the business. Therefore a genuine personal message of thanks will bolster respect for you and reinforce their engagement with the business.

Always say "Thank you", "Good work", or "Well done" when it's deserved.

Acknowledgement of good work is a powerful motivator of engagement and encourages more of the same.

Consultants will tell you that a simple "thank you" is one of the most important motivators that you can employ to make people feel good about themselves and their work. It's quick, simple and costs nothing. The only real rule that you should follow is to make sure that you don't say it frivolously. Actively look for opportunities to employ it. Where appropriate, don't hesitate to do so publicly or to let the person's immediate superior know about it.

Always make sure that the members of your team feel acknowledged.

People will be more engaged in their work when they are acknowledged for their efforts.

A happy team is a productive team. Everyone enjoys the experience of being recognized for their contributions. It provides a validation of their expertise in a way that encourages further positive effort. This can be accomplished in many different ways. A simple "thank you" should be your first choice as it provides an immediate effect. Often on longer term work this is impractical so use a standard performance review process to make sure that the information is captured and that the feedback is provided. Look for different methods depending on the circumstances and types of work. Perhaps an award of some kind is appropriate or promulgate their work in internal communications. Irrespective of the method used, it's important to ensure that the end result is that the person involved feels valued.

Tell your employees when they do well. Thinking it and saying it are two different things.

Providing feedback to a team is essential. Positive reinforcement drives improved engagement but only if the message is delivered in a way that is clearly understood.

Providing feedback on positive performance is some of the most important communication you can have with your team. Whenever the opportunity presents itself, take advantage of it. Don't make the assumption that there is some form of unspoken understanding or that 'they know'. Always err on the side of caution and make the feedback explicit. Celebrate success and make a big deal of the positive impact that it has across the entire team and the business.

Mention it in meetings, send it to group emails, blog about it and generally spread it around.

Knowledge

The 'Knowledge' characteristic represents traits that can be more easily learned as a leader.

That is to say other characteristics such as 'Quality' and 'Attitude' are things that need to be understood and developed over longer periods of time. Knowledge can be thought of as the 'tricks of the trade' that allow you to employ traits involved with communication, delegation, strategy and practical elements.

A lot of what is covered in this area is common sense and you could reasonably think of the guidance in this section as being more of a series of gentle reminders.

The aspects of knowledge that we will examine are;

- Innovation
- Delegation
- Communication
- Strategy
- Being Open Minded
- Experience
- Practicality
- Observation
- Curiosity

Innovation

Being innovative is the trait that will see you take opportunities to try different things.

Innovation in the context of leadership is not just about coming up with different ideas. It's directed towards creating a culture in your team that will encourage those ideas to be attempted. In doing so it embraces the principles of experimentation, risk, and constant improvement.

Stagnation in a team environment is a sign of impending doom. Evolution of your team and the way you do things must move forward. This ensures that you remain focussed on the tasks you need to perform and you improve the way work is carried out. Put innovation into action by trying new ideas and always looking for opportunities to make life better. Keep your team thinking and more importantly, give them an opportunity to invest in the work they're doing by having a direct influence on it.

Experiment

The principal of experimentation is one that should be followed to let you try new things and to continue a process of improvement.

If there is one constant in life, it's change. With change comes the need to adapt. There will be a plethora of ways to adapt, but deciding which one will be the most effective can only ultimately be determined by trying different things. Sure you can theorise and extrapolate from known data, but there is never any substitute for actually *doing* something.

Not only does experimentation allow you and your team to adapt and improve, but the process of experimentation is one where the entire team has an opportunity to provide input to the potential direction and in so doing, buy into the outcome. Ultimately it's an opportunity to try new things. People naturally enjoy this if they have ownership.

Don't mistake experimentation for an excuse to try a never-ending series of options and ignore what you're trying to achieve. Do due diligence by making sure that the process has structure and set goals and time-lines. Ensure that any experiment has its results documented. You need to achieve something that allows others to build on the outcome.

Although I mention it in a separate guide, remember that it's an **experiment**. It does not guarantee success or failure. The only certainty is that you should learn something. The prospect of this alone should justify the effort before you begin.

Initiate positive changes.

This proposition tells us that wherever possible you need to be the initiator of changes for the better.

If you are leading a team it's your responsibility to look for opportunities to make things better. More importantly you need to be the person who begins the process of making that change happen. The world is full of people who can put forward great ideas for improvement. The majority of them won't follow through with those ideas for one reason or another. That's not to say that the ideas aren't good, it's just to say that they may not have the opportunity or motivation to put those ideas into action. As a leader **you** need to be the person who can identify a good idea (wherever the source) and to start the process of making it happen. This doesn't mean that you have to do all the work. In the best case scenario one of your team members will come up with a great idea which makes for an ideal opportunity to invest them with the responsibility to make it happen. Support them and guide them.

Even without glorious success, experimentation is a valuable process.

Experimentation by itself has the potential to deliver positive change. But the process of experimentation has ancillary benefits that aid in encouraging a strong team.

The process of experimentation is how we learn. The experience of doing something and gaining insights from it is extremely valuable for an organisation and for the people in it. Getting your team to experiment sends them several intrinsic messages.

- You believe in their abilities to carry out a task.
- You think that they're smart.
- You want them to learn and develop themselves.

It's important to realise that all of these positive messages occur whether or not the experiment is successful.

The best creative solutions should come from your team, not from you.

Solutions to problems should come from all sources. There is no monopoly on good ideas so it stands to reason that solving problems in a team environment will have the majority of the input coming from your team.

Problem solving is something of an art form and those who know how to do it well will understand that each of us is a product of our experiences. The addition of different experiences and ways of thinking will therefore supply a wider range of potential solutions. Your team members should be the people who are most familiar with their work and the nuances that are associated with it. They are in a better position to be able to evaluate different approaches and probabilities of success. Listen to them and when assigning the task for solving a problem, the person who came up with a solution will be best motivated to implement it successfully. That may not *always* be appropriate, but it's worth keeping in mind. Lastly, don't be fixated on *your* solution being the best one. You will have a strong influence on how a problem is approached but unless you're the one doing the work, remember that yours is one opinion amongst many.

Conducting an experiment is time well spent, even if the result disappoints you.

Experiments exist as an opportunity for improvement both of processes and for individuals personally. Even if an experiment fails to produce the desired results, the intrinsic gains to the individuals involved in the exercise are still beneficial.

The process of experimentation is a voyage of discovery in the sense that the process has started without clear indication of what the final result will be. It follows therefore that the possibility exists that the result will not be what was anticipated or desired. This is not the end of the world. What should be realised is that experiments are opportunities for learning. Individuals who go through the process of experimentation are helping themselves develop and in so doing becoming more valuable to the organisation and fulfilling an internal desire to improve. Often the process of experimentation can be regarded as fun. Sometimes assigning experimental tasks to team members can be used as a form of reward. Always remember that at the end of a period of experimentation any results determined should be documented so that a wider audience can learn from the process. If those results do not support your initial aim, that doesn't mean that working through the experiment has been a failure. Think of it as an opportunity to review and improve.

Delegation

Delegating tasks is the process of apportioning bodies of work to your team members for the purposes of managing workload.

Tasks are frequently larger than any single person can reasonably carry out on their own. There may also be time constraints that demand a lengthy task be carried out hastily. Delegation allows you to divide up a job into manageable chunks. Then you can provide an opportunity to balance the workload or distribute expertise in a more granular fashion.

There are plenty of nuances to delegation. It could be employed to complete out a job quickly, to spread skills in different areas or to develop responsibility. There will always be a strong desire in leaders to just 'do it themselves'. **RESIST THIS URGE.** Develop the skill sets in your team so that they become more accomplished and enjoy their work more.

Break a complex, urgent problem into chunks, one for each of your team to solve.

The ability to delegate is a vital skill for any leader. It involves being able to break a problem into sections that can then be distributed for individual team members to work on.

More importantly a leader needs to know *how* to break a task into *manageable* portions and how to ensure that the load involved in carrying out a task is spread in a way that their team can carry it out with other tasks that are occurring simultaneously. You could be forgiven for thinking that the ability to delegate is more of a management function. However there is a significant aspect to delegation that a leader must be capable of carrying out. They must be able to recognise the skills and strengths of the individual team members as well as the load that each team member is currently working under. They must also be comfortable assigning tasks to individual team members. This might sound like a simple thing to do but many people are reluctant to assign work to others where they know they can do the job themselves. As a leader it is your responsibility to make sure that your team is working to fulfil its mission. This means being able to manage the workload using your team's skills.

For each task, assign it to an individual, or ask for a volunteer. A crowd won't take an action.

When delegating work it's important to make sure that there is a clear sense of responsibility in the individuals undertaking the tasks.

Specifics matter when giving direction and assigning work. Always make sure that your team members have a clear understanding of who is responsible for what work. If there is any doubt about who is responsible for something then by default nobody will be responsible for it. It's always better to have a volunteer for a task than to have to direct someone to carry it out. That way you can make the assumption that you will have somebody who is motivated and enthusiastic about carrying it out successfully. If assigning tasks in a meeting situation, ensure that there is a record of the meeting and that it is promulgated so that the areas of responsibility are clear.

Communication

Communication is about being able to effectively exchange information.

The most important aspect of communication in a leadership role is to remember that it's a two way thing. Giving information is just as important as receiving information. The second most important part of communication is that it's a process, not an event. It should be a feedback loop that allows all parties to ensure that the correct information has been delivered and received accurately.

Communication is a big deal. Libraries of books have been published dealing with this single trait. Effective communication is a vital tool for a leader and one that you will need to master. This doesn't mean that you need to be able to stand up in front of a crowd and give a rousing speech, but it does mean that you need to be able to get your message across accurately and to be able to receive information as it is intended by the person giving it. This trait has a vast amount of cross-over with others as there are a wide range of activities that depend on it.

Give good advice

Giving advice is the process of providing an opinion based on your experience and expertise to help others.

It might sound like something of an obvious statement but giving good advice is an important aspect of a leader's role. Your team members have a degree of focus on their work which you do not have. However, you have a broader understanding of a wider range of activities. This makes it possible for you to use your experience to help others. Giving good advice might sound like a difficult thing to achieve consistently, but the phrase is as much about letting you know that you should be confident about providing advice as a reminder to ensure that your advice isn't **bad**. Bad advice could be characterised as advice where you were uncertain about how valid it was or advice that was unrequested or poorly timed. Don't feign certainty if you are unsure and be careful about giving advice if it could be construed as unhelpful. Unhelpful advice would be the sort of thing that was done in retrospect for the purposes of highlighting someone else's failures.

Successful discussions happen in person. Context is lost over phone or email.

It is easiest to convey information via a face to face conversation as opposed to voice or text. To ensure the best chance for correct meaning to be exchanged, a discussion in person is preferred.

If you've ever been misinterpreted when having a discussion with somebody over the phone or via an email then you will understand that the better way to pass on understanding is via a face to face meeting. That's because human beings have evolved to communicate by using a range of different means, including the subtle nuances of inflection and body language that can convey information that will be lost in mediums that do not allow these clues to be expressed. The reason that emojis have become popular is that they allow additional meaning and context to be added to what otherwise is a very dry medium in print. Likewise talking via the phone does not provide the opportunity to interpret visual cues which can allow greater understanding of what the talker and indeed the listener are saying and understanding. In order of degrees of increasing legibility, email is the worst, a phone conversation is the second worst and a conversation in person is the best. Additionally, people are far more likely to be supportive in person than they will be via email or on the phone.

Be a valuable addition to any discussion or disengage. Don't be bored. Don't be boring.

Being bored or being boring is a waste of resources. Time is one of the most valuable resources you have. Ensure that you are always adding value.

If you're bored it's a sign that you are not getting value out of a situation. You need to recognise when it's happening and develop a technique for getting the conversation back on track. If you're *being* boring you need to stay alert for the signs in the audience around you that it's occurring and you need to be self aware enough to change the track of your conversation so that it adds value to the topic being discussed. If you've simply slipped into an area where people listening to you aren't interested in what you're saying, this happens and you will need to find a way to adapt your messaging. If you find that your manner or means of communication is naturally boring then you will need to be open minded enough to take steps to try and improve your way of communicating with people. The key in these situations is to try and constantly review the value you are adding.

Listen

Listening is about being able to make sure that when someone is trying to communicate something with you that you don't just *hear* what they're saying but that you *understand* what they're saying.

Listening can obviously be thought of as the act of hearing someone when they talk but actually it's as much about making sure that *any* form of communication being used is being understood clearly. A common misconception about leadership is that a leader is required to project their thoughts for others. In reality listening is about being less focused on yourself and more focused on your surroundings. Being a leader is about being able to make decisions and give directions based on a broad range of knowledge. To gain that knowledge you need to be able to gather information effectively. Encourage clarity in your team and pay attention to what they're saying. Listening effectively enables a transition between being *able* to do things and doing things.

Have difficult conversations as soon as possible.

Dealing with problems should be done without delay. When working through an issue where one or more parties will feel uncomfortable, it is better to be open, honest and to act as soon as practical. Delays in dealing with uncomfortable situations can often exacerbate a problem or start to reduce options for dealing with them sooner and mitigating their effects.

No-one likes giving or receiving bad news. When you need to get involved in a conversation that will be difficult, ensure that you have your facts straight and initiate it as soon as practical. Delaying it provides opportunity for the situation to escalate out of your control or to deteriorate to a state that will require greater correction. Be up front about the issue. Wherever possible, work with all parties to treat the problem objectively and as a process that needs to be dealt with, in the best way possible under the circumstances. Ensure that your communication is clear and unambiguous, but keep it appropriate to the situation. Where necessary document the outcomes as a record for future review. Especially in situations where you are correcting substandard behaviour.

Strategy

Strategic thinking is the implementation of decisions or plans that have a longer term benefit to business outcomes.

The key component in thinking strategically is to realise that as a leader you need to be able to guide your team towards longer term success. This will mean making sure that your priorities are focused on thinking into the future. Set good foundations and standards so that the future of your team is clear and stable.

Don't confuse strategy and tactics. Tactics are what will allow you to achieve short term victories. Strategy will help you prioritise choices so that the big picture is addressed and will allow you to win the war.

Pick your battles. Fight injustice before annoyance.

Making sure that you pick your battles is about prioritising what's important. Recognise and make the distinction between those tasks that need immediate attention and those that can be dealt with as time allows.

Understanding prioritisation is a vital skill. The distinction between injustice and annoyance illustrates the subtle differences in the way problems present themselves. You may be highly motivated to correct an annoyance but the bigger picture is to fight injustice. This will often be a trade-off between short term and long term needs. Focus on the long game whilst managing short term requirements. For the record, if genuine injustice presents itself, it is your responsibility to make **sure** that you deal with it swiftly and appropriately.

It's vital to have a vision, but you've got to have a plan.

To be able to achieve goals for yourself and your team you need to be able to formalise a direction and to have that direction documented.

A vision is an aspirational goal, a plan is a method by which you can carry out a task. Everyone needs to know where they're heading. You need to know and your team needs to know. A vision doesn't have to be a concrete goal. It could be as loosely defined as "happiness" or "being more productive". A plan will set out the steps that you need in order to achieve that vision. Discuss the plan with your customers and your team. Get agreement on the best way forward and prioritise your tasks appropriately.

Build your team with people who you would trust with your life.

Wherever and whenever possible you should recruit people to work for you who you can have complete trust in.

This principle sounds slightly dramatic but it underlies the need to have trust in your team members. Building a team needs to be done carefully. While there will always be a requirement to ensure that new personnel have the required skills, it is arguably more important that they possess the right attitude. Smart, motivated people will always be in demand. It's important that you ensure that the workplace is conducive to supporting them so that they can continue to grow and develop. Look after your team members and they will look after you.

If something is broken it should be fixed right away. If it can wait maybe you don't need it.

If something is wrong in the workplace it should get immediate attention. If it's something that doesn't need immediate attention it should be examined to confirm whether it's really needed or not.

Often we perpetuate systems or ways of carrying out work that are historic in nature and therefore we can lose track of how important they are to our business. We should constantly go through a cycle of review to ensure the relevance of any tasks we carry out to maintain efficiencies. It's hard to do this while systems are operating but if for any reason they stop operating it's an ideal opportunity to pause, reflect and evaluate relevance. It's not true that everything can be fixed straight away. Even those systems which can be regarded as critical. Managing priorities in the workplace will continue to be a topic that you'll have to deal with on a case by case basis.

If you have an emergency every day, then an emergency means nothing.

If all your work is high priority, labelling something as urgent has no meaning.

The problem being described in this area is that if everything you do is rushed then rushed is normal. This would be symptomatic of a team that was incorrectly resourced and it should be corrected. Basically you're working too hard. Your team needs opportunities to carry out their work in an environment where the expectation is that they can respond to normal requests in a professional way.

Rushing work does not provide the opportunity for staff members to do their best on a job. In emergency situations team members are less likely to carry out important actions associated with tasks like documentation, peer review, building in resilience or performing due diligence on work. You are basically building a house of cards. Everyone wants to do good work and without the ability to take appropriate care they will feel as if they're not doing their best. In an *actual* emergency the rules and the expectations are different.

If more than one person is responsible for a task then no-one is responsible.

This tells us that assigning responsibility must be done at an individual scale so that there is clear direction and expectations for all parties.

The first thing that should be cleared up is that in this instance the concept of individual responsibility is not intended to be describing *moral* responsibility. Instead, it is about clarity for all parties involved in work, in knowing where their responsibilities lie in order to ensure that work is completed satisfactorily. If two people are assigned a task, neither can be reasonably expected to assume that they are responsible for its completion. It can easily be argued that they *share* some responsibility but the problem is that there is no clarity about where that distinction lies. Therefore, in order to ensure the instructions are unambiguous, it is important that each individual knows what their individual responsibilities are. This is as important for a leader as it is for a team member. It provides a leader with clear lines of communication to ensure that work is progressing satisfactorily and it provides each team member with clarity of expectations.

The reason that this falls into the strategic area is that it's very easy to provide direction to a group so that it has the *appearance* of work been assigned appropriately. But in the long term there is no guarantee that the right people know what is expected of them.

A leader knows when to set aside important things in order to accomplish vital ones.

Be aware of what's **truly** important in carrying out the tasks assigned to your team.

This may be a matter of prioritisation or simply identifying what matters most in any particular situation. The ability to do this effectively will improve with time and experience in any role but it is dependent on ensuring that you constantly develop your knowledge of your team and business. It's easy to get drawn into thinking that you're doing the right thing at the right time when in reality you're serving internal prejudices. Constantly look to the future and ensure that the goals you're focusing on are the important ones for the long term.

Being Open Minded

Being open minded is the trait of being able to consider things that might go against your natural preconceptions.

An open minded approach to leadership occurs when a leader is willing to consider new approaches and to listen and take note of different opinions. It requires you to be able to identify biases that you might harbour and to be able to consider options on their true merits.

Some may think that the role of leadership and alternative thinking to be mutually exclusive. However, nothing could be further from the truth. It's important to remember that the art of good leadership is being able to move your team in the right direction. Being able to consider all the options available objectively and without prejudice is a key to making sure that you can draw on as wide a collection of knowledge as possible. This doesn't mean abdicating your responsibility to lead, but accepting the fact that you aren't the sole source of solutions.

There is a time to use a hierarchical structure and there is a time to allow a community approach.

A hierarchical command structure and a flat collaborative environment are both useful methods of getting good results from teams. They are significantly different and therefore they are applicable in different environments and situations. Use a hierarchical structure when you need to ensure clear lines of responsibility and decision making and utilise a flat structure in situations where you want to encourage responsibility and free communication across the board.

There's a good reason why the military use a hierarchical structure to maintain their armed forces. There is a clear line of authority with a devolution of responsibility that allows groups with set tasks to know what is expected of them and how to do it. There is a reduced opportunity for deviation away from the required objective and a common clarity of purpose. This is useful when boundaries need to be set and maintained and where fixed goals and methods are expected. A flat structure reduces the lag in internal communications and provides opportunities to draw a range of information from disparate sources. Decision making is pushed out to allow a more flexible response. The task that your organisation has, or the conditions under which you operate will be key drivers in determining which approach you take.

Respect and seek to understand the views of people who are different from you.

Diversity is a strong enabler of innovation and problem solving. Having access to a wide range of viewpoints and ways of thinking expands options for greater efficiencies.

Always look for opportunities to do things better. Different ideas and viewpoints make for opportunities to see things in different ways and to find solutions that you won't have considered. Don't fall into the trap of thinking of diversity as some kind of reaction to an imbalance of representation of any one group or another. It is a genuine mechanism for adding value to a team. As a leader you should always look for opportunities to improve the diversity of your group. It's just good business. At the same time make an effort to change your own thinking to expand your options. No one individual or group has a monopoly on good ways of working. Use diverse thinking to improve your skill set and to understand your team better.

It's not your job to come up with all the ideas yourself. Ask for suggestions.

Leading a team means accepting responsibility for people with a wide range of skills and abilities. This is a repository of knowledge that can be employed to best effect by involving them in decision making processes and using their input as a resource.

Think of your team as an extension of your knowledge base. They are a resource that you can use to augment your thinking. You will never have a monopoly on good ideas and to think so would be the height of hubris. Encourage an open exchange of information between your team members and to yourself. Look for opportunities to recognise valuable input and to promote it. Directly ask for suggestions. Use problems as opportunities for demonstrating variety of thought. Don't marginalise thinking that you don't understand. Ask for explanations.

Remember what your mission is, but be ready to change.

A leader has a responsibility to ensure that the needs of the business are being maintained and that tasks that are required of them are being completed. They need to remain focussed on this as their priority but stay ready to adapt and change as required to meet changing business needs.

Know what your mission is. Put it on the wall, remind yourself and your team of it and prosecute it with vigour. This should be standard practice for ensuring the visibility and relevance of what you do on a day to day basis. At the same time always remember that plans change. Commit to action, but don't be surprised if there is a need to pivot in response to changing requirements. The need to accept change and be ready to implement it should be baked into your team's culture. When the need arises, review, confirm and commit.

Be prepared to disagree with a decision, but commit to supporting it.

Solutions can take many forms. There will be a range of possible approaches and an acceptable solution is *still* solution. Irrespective of whether a new approach comes from you or any other member of your team it must be endorsed and actioned.

You don't have a monopoly on good ideas and there will be more than one solution to pretty much any problem. It's expected that any action should be debated to determine the right approach. Part of that process may well include you disagreeing with the method to be used. That's fine. Robust discussion of the possibilities is healthy and necessary. Be respectful of all involved. Accept going in, that your solution may not be the one that will ultimately be used. You don't *need* to agree with it, it just needs to be effective. Once the approach is fixed, back it wholeheartedly.

You don't have a monopoly on good ideas.

Leaders have a responsibility to ensure that good practices are followed and that solutions to problems are enacted. The source of the solutions should be agnostic.

Your ideas are not automatically the best ideas. Your team and the wider environment are resources that you can use to source solutions. Make sure that you put aside any preconception that stops you considering a wider set of options. That includes consideration of ideas from outside your team. Take care to avoid any bias and be open minded about learning new ways of doing business.

Some team members are subject matter experts. Remember to ask for their input.

A team will have experts in diverse areas. Recognise their specialist skills and consult them when work in those situations occurs.

It might seem like obvious advice, but use your best resources to best effect. It can be tempting to make decisions on the fly, based on your own broad overview, but your subject matter experts will have a depth of understanding that will only come with their long standing experience in their specialist field. They will notice things that you won't see and will bring options to the table that you won't have thought of. Always remember to give credit where it is due.

Don't let a team member's age prejudice you to their skill level (younger or older).

Age and experience are poor indicators to capability. The value in a potential team member can be more accurately measured in enthusiasm, attitude, cleverness and willingness to learn.

Age is no indicator of value to a team. There are a range of other characteristics that you can evaluate that demonstrate capability. First amongst this is passion. Any person who is passionate about what they do for a job should go on your short-list. How do they approach learning? Do they wait to be told to go on a course or are they trying new things just for the sake of it? Are they clever? Can they form a sound argument and frame complex concepts into easy to understand descriptions? Is their attitude positive? Do they want to be there and look for positive aspects to their work? Any one of these is a better indicator of suitability than either being younger or older than you would expect.

Don't continue a practice just because that's the way it's always been done.

Maintaining consistency is an important consideration in carrying out tasks, but always question practices to ensure that they remain relevant and fit for purpose.

Doing the same thing time and again is ignoring the tendency for change in your environment to have altered the conditions you are working under. It's easy to become complacent about processes and to be lulled into a false sense of security that what you are doing is still being done in the best way. Constantly review your practices and encourage your team to challenge the way that the group does business.

Don't be too proud to ask for help, even from people you dislike.

Asking for assistance is a sign of acceptance of the reality that no one person can know everything. Asking for help is using the resources available.

It can feel a bit like an admission of failure to ask for help. But if you're honest with yourself it is a greater example of failure to have to go through a learning process that someone else has already suffered through. Even if you struggle with the fact that you don't know everything, it is often a great way to initiate good communication to use a simple question. Think of it as an opportunity to improve a relationship. If you are in the situation where you don't have a great relationship with the person you are asking it will be a development experience as well.

Experience

Experience is the management of acquired knowledge.

The trait of experience does not refer to time served in a leadership role. Instead, it's the gathering of information that is required for a leadership role and for the team. It's about having realistic expectations of yourself, your team and your organisation by taking the time to experience and learn their capabilities.

As a leader you need to have an intimate understanding of the functions of your unit and the capabilities your team. This cannot be gained by assuming from prior knowledge or from third hand reports. You need to be involved at a level where you can gain a first hand appreciation of what's going on. This doesn't mean losing yourself by working at a job that you shouldn't be doing. That's what your team is for. Your job is to *understand* what they're doing so that you can manage the needs of the business in line with the capabilities of your team.

The important things in life will never be formally tested.

The process of testing is to discover if a person is able to provide a suitable response to an objective proposition. This is a valuable mechanism to determine the ability of a person to respond in a predictable and appropriate way. However, the process of testing is an artificial construct where there is a degree of safety and other restrictions built in. A person's ability to deal with situations that have no solution or which aren't able to be simulated are a better indicator of their capability because the nature of the experience is a true reflection of how a person will respond in similar situations.

Testing provides an objective measure for comparison. This is a good method of evaluating capability. A person's character is arguably more important than their capability and testing that is a difficult proposition. Only the lifelong responses to real world situations will demonstrate a person's honesty, courage, integrity or loyalty. Use formal testing for determining measureable characteristics. Does a person have a degree? Do they know how to create a financial spreadsheet? When you want to actually know what a person is like, you will need to spend time with them and ask the people who have worked with them. Use your instincts to guide how you go about determining character. Ask for others to consider the question and provide a different viewpoint.

Keep a record of your work. Clarity will come from writing it down

Good documentation is a central tenet of professional work. The two fundamental aspects of this are creating a historical record and creating a reference. The historical record will allow you to recall a sequence of events, assist in fault finding and create a record of governance. Reference documentation provides a single point of truth for yourself and others to use as a knowledge base.

The modern framework for capturing information electronically is using the equivalent of blogs and Wikis. There are more than one variation of both, but the principles remain the same. A blog will provide a timestamped record of day to day activities that allows retrieval of what has occurred in the past. This makes looking for triggers that could be causing faults or trends that might indicate problems, much easier. Wikis are designed to provide a reference point for knowledge. Even if a standard way of doing something might change, regularly updating the Wiki page for it, means that the 'standard' can always be found in one place. Documenting information reliably is something of a cultural practice. It's one that you should strongly encourage as a leader. It acts as a force multiplier to allow a range of people to get access to information that would otherwise be left to the inaccuracies of individual memories

Gain a realistic understanding of what your team and organisation can and cannot do.

Having an understanding of the capabilities of your team is a fundamental requirement so that you can manage tasks and workload. This will take time and will require working with your wider team to establish limitations and capacity. The key is to ensure that this understanding is based on the *actual* capabilities, not those that are either published or desired.

There are two aspects to this proposition that are important to consider. The first is understanding the work that is being carried out and the second is to ensure that what you know is realistic. Understanding the abilities of your team and organisation is something that can first be established by examining the business drivers that are applied to both and the resources that are employed to achieve them. From there you need to review how that theoretical model is put into practise in the real world. To do that you need to spend time getting to know your team and your customers. Get an honest appraisal of how the team is performing and where its strengths and weaknesses lie. Make sure that you use this information wisely to plan and commit to work that can be realistically carried out and avoid overcommitting.

Don't assume anything is possible or impossible until you've asked the people who will do the job.

A leader will have access to the expertise and experience of their team. They are the resource that can be used to make sure that any strategic and tactical planning is practical.

It's very easy in a leadership position to make assumptions on the practicality of different approaches to work or tasks. While you should have a good grasp of the capabilities of your group you aren't expected to understand the intricacies of every part of it. That makes it difficult to predict problems or opportunities that are evident to those who are actually doing the work. Try to avoid committing to significant tasks without consulting with your experts. They are as much invested in making sure that the work is successful as you are.

Ensure that every system has the required documentation so that it can be repaired manually.

Systems are naturally complex and require expertise to develop and maintain. Distributing that expertise using good documentation allows others to develop skills and knowledge that enhance business continuity.

Documentation is often neglected or avoided for various reasons. Part of your role is to ensure that your team has the opportunity and the motivation to provide good documentation about the systems they work on. That documentation supports a number of outcomes. Firstly it means that you are spreading your corporate knowledge to a wider audience. This allows better supportability. Secondly your team is improving their professional development through access to more knowledge. Lastly you are providing good governance of the organization and the services it provides.

Know how all your systems work at a high level.

A leader needs to have a broad understanding of the work that is carried out by their group. This allows them to allocate resources appropriately and prioritize to support the wider business.

You need to know about the things you are responsible for. It's easy to let your experts get on with things and when things are going well that's great. However you also have to understand what they are doing in a broader sense. Team work is fundamentally about multiple people working together to achieve common goals. Part of the effort required involves orchestrating and guiding the process. This requires a good understanding of the parts that make up the whole without needing to know all the details. Your job is to see the components that make up the bigger picture.

Be the information hub. Help connect the dots that wouldn't otherwise get connected

A leader needs to *be* well informed and to keep *others* well informed. They need to be a conduit for information and to be regarded as the primary point of contact for ensuring that the big picture is understood.

You need to know what's going on and to return the favour by letting everyone know what's happening. Gathering information will give you the opportunity to understand the bigger picture and more importantly it will allow you to make connections between different events or processes that might not necessarily be obvious when considering only a subset of information. Just as important as being able to collate and evaluate data from a wide range of sources, you need to cultivate and promote yourself as the **right** person to receive information. This will be reinforced by being able to provide good feedback and insights. Make sure to distribute knowledge widely, acknowledge your sources and give credit where it is due.

The more you do, the more you *can* do.

A leader can be expected to be constantly expanding their horizons by stepping outside their comfort zone and working on new things in new ways. This will continually grow their repertoire of skills and knowledge while looking to improve and advance. The more the boundaries can be pushed, the greater the ability to develop more skills.

Evolution as a leader is important. You need to be able to recognise the need to change and adapt. Part of that process is exposing yourself to different work and ideas so that you can discover new ways of doing business and learn how to improve. There is no better way to learn something than by *doing* it. Actively seek out opportunities to 'have a go' at something different. Often these experiences will be challenging. In fact they *should* be challenging so that your skill set is constantly expanded. The greater your exposure to new activities, the more capable you become and by extension the greater your ability to lead and help others.

Leadership cannot realistically be taught. It must be learned.

The act of leading is one where a person accepts and embraces the opportunity to lead. It **must** be driven by desire to be successful. Teaching people to lead provides them with tools, but they need to *want* to learn so that they can put it into action.

This is not an exercise in nature vs nurture. A person can learn how to be an effective leader and/or they can have a natural flair for it. What needs to be understood is that no amount of teaching someone how to lead will be effective if they don't have a desire to learn how to lead. This is especially important for you as a developing leader. Going on courses is useful, but realise that this isn't a substitute for effective learning. Pay attention to your surroundings. Listen to people. Go out of your way to put yourself into positions to develop your skills. Get a mentor. Continually work to improve.

Your organisation is only as good as the people you recruit.

The people who make up your organization *are* your organization. Recruiting the right people is the best method to influence the future of your business.

Hiring staff is a very important activity. Always remember that they will be the future of your business. They will need to *want* to be part of that future to add maximum value and your job is to ensure that you hire people with that desire. There will always be specific skill sets that you need to target, but there are also general ones that you should identify and covet. Look for people who are enthusiastic and want to learn. Find people who are willing to accept responsibility and to help others. Look for *good* people that reflect the qualities of what you want your business to be.

Practicality

Being practical describes techniques for getting things done in the real world.

A practical leader is someone who understands how to put the theoretical techniques required for leadership into practice. This will include understanding the distinction *between* the theory and practice.

As a leader you need to be realistic about how you work with your team and external customers to accomplish goals. Often this will mean establishing that, while there is an ideal way to carry out a task, there is also a gulf between what *should* be done and what *can* be done. You should also be able to make sure that in the process of carrying out your role that you make the most efficient use of the time and resources of the team and yourself.

Allow yourself some time alone. It will help you think.

Considering difficult problems demands concentration. Removing distractions will provide options for clarity of thinking.

Taking time by yourself is a valuable tool to help consider difficult problems. The hustle and bustle of day to day activities is part of looking after the team and doing business. But part of your work will mean considering complex tasks that demand thinking deeply. To do this you will want to be able to remove yourself from distractions. Part of the aim is to avoid the cognitive lag that occurs with context switching. The mind is very good at holding complex information in a 'ready state' so that it can be processed. However, when a competing activity is introduced (with a request on a different topic for instance) the mind switches to address the new request and the complex information that it is holding is disturbed. When you subsequently return to the original problem it will take time to return to the original depth of thinking. This is obviously a waste of your time and therefore something to avoid.

Time is your most valuable commodity. Use it wisely.

Time is a finite resource. It can't be created or bought. Manage it via realistic forecasting and assigning milestones with time-frames.

You only get so much time to carry out your tasks. This is true personally as a leader and for your team. Time needs to be managed carefully and husbanded as a resource. Don't waste it and don't take it for granted. Beware of the little things that happen often that should be eliminated to save time. Things like useless emails or social media alerts. Carefully manage social interactions. These are necessary to maintain a stable social environment, but they need to be watched and moderated if necessary. Plan your allocation of time so that you can keep track of your resource. Set realistic time-frames for work and monitor your progress against your plan. You should harbour a small discretionary reserve to use for emergencies. Lastly, take care not to waste other people's time as well. It is the height of poor form.

Your knowledge is a resource that others can draw from, not a treasure to hoard for yourself

A leader will be someone who develops a sound understanding of their role and the intricacies of carrying it out successfully. They should also have a very good appreciation of the activities that they are responsible for as well as disseminating this knowledge clearly and widely.

Empowering and developing your team should be second nature. Do that by sharing knowledge and by encouraging others to do the same. You should always be open by default. Look for ways to make information available at all times. Make sure that your team understands that you have the same expectation of them. Open information has a critical mass. Keep persevering and distributing until it becomes a self perpetuating thing. You will never be respected for holding knowledge to yourself but you will be admired for making an effort to inform and help others.

Expecting people to work long hours is wrong in many ways.

Each employee should have an agreed set of working conditions which will include hours of work. There may be occasions where they will be asked to work additional hours or there may be an emergency situation where they will respond to a call outside of business hours. Whatever the situation, these events should be regarded as out of the ordinary and the employees should be remunerated appropriately. Working longer hours impacts on health and well-being. It may be tolerable in the short-term but it is not sustainable. If it is happening regularly then this indicates a lack of resourcing.

Working excessive hours has a detrimental effect on people's health. There is a need to ensure that your staff balance their working life and their personal life. That will mean different things to different people depending on the situation and the roles they are filling. Whatever the situation, if you are expecting them to exceed their agreed time at work then you will be in violation of their trust. Your job is to make sure that you look after your team and keep them healthy and productive. Exceeding their working hours places pressure on them in their personal life and increases their exposure to situations where their health may be at risk. If you find yourself in a situation where you have employees working excessive hours take a critical look at your resources to see where they are deficient.

If you want to make things you're going to have to get your hands dirty.

The process of getting things done and creating things means applying yourself to the task. This is a metaphor for getting your hands dirty. No amount of planning and strategizing can make a product. Do due diligence on preparing, but don't be afraid of getting started and putting planning into practice.

Doers do. It's a really simple sentence but it's far more difficult to understand what it means. There is an inherent caution in carrying out practical work. Whether that is as simple as a common task or as complex as a major project. The risk associated with moving from planning to reality manifests itself as a move from security to the unknown. Planning *reduces* risk. Implementation *introduces* risk. Moving from one to the other is mentally difficult. Be aware that as a leader you are responsible for adequate planning *and* for accepting the risk of doing practical work. The more often you get your hands dirty, the better you will understand the connection between preparation and practice. Don't fear it, use it as a way to improve your ability to get things done. Help those around you understand how to accept responsible risks and to make things happen. Don't despair **when** things go wrong. They will occasionally. Use your flexibility to work through problems and resolve them.

In order to deliver projects you need to finish them.

A leader is responsible for the delivery of tasks against a business plan. Have clearly defined deliverables and work them to completion. Work that exceeds the deliverables are different / new bodies of work and should have new delivery deadlines.

Be 'results focused' in the sense that you are employed to deliver to an agreed schedule. Take that seriously and make sure that the team takes it seriously as well. This is delivering to your customer's requirements. Use those goals and deadlines as the finishing line for bodies of work. Success and satisfying your customer's needs is measured by reaching those finishing lines. Don't get distracted from those agreed goals. Publish them prominently and refer to them often. Use them to build your team's reputation as 'finishers'.

Finishing things is the difference between being busy and being productive.

Delivering on bodies of work means achieving goals and milestones that are agreed beforehand. If you're not working towards agreed goals then you aren't going to finish anything. Your performance can only be measured against achieved goals.

Being busy is great. In fact it's *really* important. But it doesn't count for much if you're not achieving anything. Meeting goals and milestones is the way that you provide verification that you're working successfully to accomplish your organisation's mission. Justifying your activities is simple and self evident when you're finishing tasks. Publish your goals prominently and use them to focus activity to ensure that 'busy' ends up being productive.

There is no better way of learning something than doing it.

The application of a skill set is a learning experience. As much as practise is designed to prepare people for using a skill in the real world, actually *doing* the job is the best way to reinforce any training and accelerate full understanding.

Learning is a process to impart skills and experience to allow someone to carry out a task. It is not an end in itself. Don't let apprehension defer using the skills for real. Take the appropriate time to provide effective training and use testing to confirm understanding and preparedness. Confirm that training is effective by reviewing once trainees have been in the role. However, don't underestimate the value of letting people use on the job training to learn. This needs to be done in a safe and controlled environment to mitigate risk, but it presents an effective learning opportunity.

Standard procedures are just suggestions.

Standard procedures serve the purpose of setting a consistent way of carrying out a task. These are enormously useful to improve efficiency and effectiveness but they should not be confused with policy. They represent a best practice solution and should always be viewed as the best *current* solution. Wherever possible take the opportunity to improve them.

You should always strive to incorporate standard operating procedures into your business. They are an effective way to bring consistency to carrying out repetitive tasks. However, they are also just the best *known* way of doing a job. Capture your procedures in such a way that promotes easy amendment and improvement. A wiki style of documentation fits the need well but whatever mechanism you use, actively promote it as being subject to constant review and improvement.

Don't attempt multitasking until you master single-tasking.

Carrying out more than one task at a time is only effective when it can be done in a way that maintains a focus on being able to complete the work successfully. Success achieving tasks one at a time should be gained before working on multiple projects.

Let's cut to the chase. If you try to do many things at once you will divide your attention and make completing the tasks more difficult. It's a common problem. People start too many programs and the work suffers. Everyone believes that they can manage the complexity until they realize that they can't. Approach this piece of advice seriously. Build a reputation as a finisher by starting and finishing one project at a time. Encourage your team to do the same. Monitor and publish your progress so that those who you report to understand the workload and can plan around your schedule. When you are completely confident that you have mastered single threaded success, think about **two** things at once.

Work should be purposeful, stimulating, and challenging. If the reasoning for it is abstract, clarify.

Team members gain meaning by understanding what is going on and how the work they are carrying out supports the larger picture. Not all immediate work can be exciting, but by providing context in a digestible form it can be purposeful.

A person who enjoys their work will be self motivated to do a good job. As a leader you should always make an effort to ensure that you align the work and the person carrying out the activity so that they are compatible. Making sure that your team know how their efforts fit into the broader context is a force multiplier. This gives their work purpose. It means that they can add value by looking at what they are doing with a view to integration with ancillary activities. If you find yourself in the situation where the purpose of the work is unclear, make an effort to clarify so that the expended effort can be enjoyed more. A useful ally in this is the organisation's business plans. These should form a hierarchy that shows how work at the lower level integrates into the organisation's goals and mission.

Run emergency drills when all is well. A genuine emergency is no time for training.

Emergency procedures exist to ensure that in the event of a problem that requires immediate action there is a clear guide on how to deal with the incident. In order to ensure that the procedures are correct and that personnel are familiar with how to react they need to be rehearsed and evaluated. These practises are essential for critical systems and safety. They require all involved to be familiar with the procedures through practise.

Emergency drills are an essential activity to ensure that when required, all concerned are able to carry out their roles quickly and safely. These drills can often be viewed in a poor light. However, they serve to ensure that when a foreseen problem occurs that people are ready to act. However, just being ready isn't enough. People need to have a familiarity developed through repetitive practise. Even if only for the purposes of confirming that such procedures are relevant and appropriate. Ensure that all procedures are appropriately documented and that training is planned (with a degree of randomness) and results (of effectiveness) published. For best effect put someone other than yourself in charge of determining the timing for drills so that you also experience the process in its genuine form.

Everybody has talents. You need to learn how to harness those talents toward the same goal.

Different people have different skill sets. Recruiting, strategy, training and planning will allow the right skills to be focussed in the right areas.

As a leader you should always be looking for ways to ensure that the right people are tasked against the right work. People should be doing work that they enjoy. It should stimulate and challenge them so that they have an intrinsic sense of worth whenever they come to work. This process starts when recruiting. Hire appropriately to the task required. When people arrive, pay attention to what their capabilities are and where their preferences lie. Train them in the areas where they require development and build this into your strategy for accomplishing the organisation's mission. It sounds really easy to say it, but this is serious strategic thinking that requires real management. Don't do any of this off the cuff.

You can't change a force of nature, but you can use the force to reach your destination.

Things happen that cannot be controlled. These events cannot be influenced and as such they will have an effect on business. The job of a leader is to shape the effect such that it guides the business in a positive way.

There will be circumstances and situations that you can't influence. While you can rail against them, try to realise that ultimately you need to accept the fact that they have happened or will occur in the future. Once you come to terms with this you need to work out how you can use the situation to the best advantage of the team and the wider business. This means mitigating the effects if necessary and then using the event to direct your work. The first step is to make sure that whatever has occurred you need to stabilise the team so that you can adequately read the situation correctly. Then you need to look for opportunities that the situation presents to use it to shape your work. This might sound a little trite, but there will always be something positive that can be discovered from less than ideal circumstances. Always remember that it is counter-productive to continue to worry about the event itself. If you can't influence it, let it go. Just worry about the effect that it has. *That* you can influence.

Observation

Being observant is about being aware of your situation and being able to evaluate it accurately.

Your power of observation is the trait that will allow you to be able to notice the world around you and more importantly to be able to see it for what it is. This means being able to see and evaluate time wastage, bullshit, and incompetence amongst other things.

Everyone develops ways that they observe their piece of the world. As a leader you will need to make evaluations about what you see so that you can deal with them for what they really are. This will mean looking critically at your environment, those you interact with and how you approach your role. In some cases this will be a skill that you learn through some hard knocks. The key is to learn and hone your observation skills.

Decisions that don't need to be made are time wasters.

Evaluate the priority and value of problems that you and your team are asked to work on. Often you will be asked to carry out evaluations that are speculative or not aligned with your business plan. If you can't justify them to your boss or the chief financial officer then you need to seriously consider whether or not you should proceed.

Your time and that of your team is assigned to a plan. That plan aligns to your business and gives your work direction and purpose. Requests for your time that fall outside of the plan should be viewed (at best) as an overhead that you will need to carry. In the worst case scenario you could be asked to involve your team in unproductive and unsanctioned work. Be careful what you agree to and carefully review your responsibilities to the business against any requests made of you. Wasting time is a bad thing. It is probably your most valuable resource. Husband your resources and use them appropriately.

Real time monitoring of your critical systems is invaluable.

Maintaining over-watch of the things that are important to you is vital to ensure that you are providing an agreed upon service within your resource limits.

Monitoring is often associated with technological systems but it is also applicable to other situations. It boils down to knowing what's important to you and knowing what the status of those things is. Maintain this visibility in real time so that when something changes you know immediately. This function is often neglected until an incident proves that it shouldn't be. In many ways it is synonymous with insurance. It requires an investment up front, betting against a situation occurring that you might rather avoid. Work hard to bake monitoring into your culture. Make it standard practice. There doesn't need to be a single all encompassing solution for every eventuality. Identify your critical systems and put something/anything in place first. Then look at how you can broaden your view. Make someone responsible for keeping an eye on it. Then when it saves your bacon publish the fact so that it promotes *more* monitoring.

Develop a reliable bullshit detector.

You will be the target of misinformation from time to time. Apply a critical thought process to evaluating the veracity of what you are told so that you can look out for instances where you are being mislead.

Instances where people flat out lie to you should be few and far between. That's not to say that it doesn't happen, but it will be rare (hopefully). More often than not if you are being mislead it will be through withholding information, or being overly optimistic / pessimistic about time-lines or capabilities. In many cases people just believe that they're on the margin of what is possible, so they're comfortable relaying it. The problem comes when they are less than forthcoming about the risks, consequences, options or percentages of success in the time available. There is a good chance that you will have an uneasy feeling in circumstances where you think you're being strung along. Trust that instinct and start asking questions. At this point you should investigate to see if time-lines are realistic, are prices known or estimated, what are the risks. It's better to be able to educate people to supply you with realistic information in the future rather than to punish poor decision making. Celebrate accuracy.

Respectful team members will solve problems together. Rude team members create problems.

The value of respect is a powerful enabler that allows people to work and interact in a way that focuses on recognising individual strengths and valuing them. Failure to act respectfully towards others promotes antagonism and division.

Working collaboratively means managing the differences between people in a positive way so that the emphasis can be put on the strengths that make teamwork effective. To do this requires individuals acknowledging each other positively. Respect in this form fosters better communication and esprit de corps. Which in turn supports greater opportunities for working together to solve problems. Failure to respect one another indicates a breakdown in teamwork which will ultimately be destructive. Be proactive about showing respect and calling out others when they don't. Set the example for others to follow. Values are particularly important to demonstrate as a leader. You are the standard that others will measure themselves by and hold themselves to.

Don't put down to ill-intent what can be attributed to incompetence.

It is extremely common to imagine that actions of others that appear misguided or wrong, in whatever way, are as the result of an intentional act. This is seldom the case and more often than not the act is one that occurred accidentally or stems from poor decision making.

Accidents and poor decision making are far more common causes of problems than malice. When looking at situations where things have gone wrong it is a natural reaction to imagine that the act was deliberately caused and / or premeditated. It has been my experience (i.e. I have no facts to back this up) that incompetence is almost always the root cause of the problem. Not that we should label the person / people involved as incompetent, but more that the circumstances that led to the failure were not correctly thought out. Certainly consider all the possible causes, but be aware that there is a possible unconscious bias to think that something that has gone wrong was deliberately planned. The simpler (and therefore more likely explanation) is that bad things happen because of bad luck or bad planning, not bad people.

Tolerate failure, not incompetence. Make sure that you know what the difference is.

Success is not guaranteed in any venture. Failure will occasionally occur. When it does, differentiate your response based on reasoning. Failure can be acceptable when understood and correctable. However, failure through inability to perform correctly (assuming a lack of competence to improve) needs to be corrected by changing the responsibilities of the people involved.

Mistakes will happen and failure is a part of life. The reasons for it are many and varied. As a leader you need to ascertain the reasons for any failure to determine how to correct it and improve. If the failure is as a result of people acting inappropriately, not in accordance with directions or because the task is fundamentally beyond them, then this is a cause for corrective action. A normal failure should be a learning experience that will result in improvement. A failure which you don't learn from, is a waste of resources and time. You can't easily assign this type of problem to an 'unfortunate circumstances' category. You can't tolerate gross and unnecessary wastage. Ensure that those involved are aware of the problem that has occurred, the waste that has resulted and the need to ensure that it doesn't happen again. It would probably be wise to ensure that the incident is noted for historical purposes in case of a repeat that might warrant more serious actions.

If you feel something's wrong, you're probably right.

The more experienced a leader becomes, the more the skill of identifying the right thing from the wrong thing becomes. Don't trust this skill without an appropriate checking process, but realise that it can be a useful indicator *or* that it can be a source of bias.

The more time and experience that you have in a leadership role the more likely you will be at being able to discern a good thing from a bad one. This isn't some form of natural instinct. Instead it's the process of being able to evaluate quickly based on previously experience. It will lack the rigour that is necessary for any significant decision, but in the absence of the opportunity to apply that rigour it is better than nothing. While you need to temper your trust of this 'instinct', you should use it as an indicator to explore further or to lead enquiries. These 'feelings' will colour your thinking. Beware of establishing a bias that blinds you to alternative options. Challenge yourself and review. However, don't be afraid of making a judgement call based on your experience.

Curiosity

Curiosity is the trait that describes a desire to learn.

To be a curious person you will naturally have a desire to pursue knowledge. This is a desirable trait for a leader and one that should be encouraged in your team members. It will directly impact on innovation in your group and by extension improve how your team members feel about their work.

Being curious has the potential to be a double edged sword. You will need to be aware of the potential for time wasting and by the same token you will need to be aware of the potential for genuine innovation and improvement. Curiosity is like a desire to innovate, but dialled down a bit. You should always be curious about your surroundings and be open to the potential for letting that lead to an opportunity and then develop into a more focussed project.

Research is formalised curiosity.

Developing and learning is a vital part of growth and development. The trait of curiosity is a symptom of the desire to know more and to improve. Encourage this trait to promote positive change.

A curious disposition is a great way to start a dive into a more meaningful process. Research and development is a crucial part of improvement for an organization but often it is tied to a formal process that requires significant structure to manage. This is not always the most agile method for encouraging change. Look for opportunities to encourage people's natural curiosity. Give them a chance to follow their noses when investigating different ways of doing business or possible improvements to products or services. If their investigations look promising start to give them structural support and encourage a more detailed approach. Try not to stymie their passion with red tape and instead give them the support that research and development deserves.

Attitude

The 'Attitude' characteristic represents the type of actions and approach that an effective leader will take to working with their team.

I've used the words '*working with*' very deliberately here since attitude isn't something that allows you to direct or manage your team. It's something that your team will see as you conduct yourself and it should allow them to have confidence in you.

The last thing that you should be considering is that by having 'attitude' you are in any way displaying some kind of bizarre gangster approach in the workplace. That would be totally the wrong direction.

The attitudes that we will examine are;

- Calmness
- Inspiration
- Motivation
- Restlessness
- Collaboration
- Self Awareness
- Positivity
- Assuredness
- Disciplined
- Aspiration

Calmness

Being calm is a trait that is displayed by not becoming overly excited or anxious in time of trouble or frustration.

As a leader a sense of calm is the rational, clear approach that your team need to see when emergencies occur. It's also what is needed when things that might cause an emotional response are dealt with in a polite, peaceful manner. This is always a good approach to modifying an uncertain situation.

Being calm as a leader is more about what you're *not* doing rather than being calm. In times of emergency, people are naturally going to be reacting in a way that will reflect the excitement of the moment. Some will struggle to process what is going on. Others will have difficulty focusing on correcting the problem. People will naturally take their cues from those around them. If you project an air of calm and being in control, that will assist them to do the same thing. The same is true for becoming overly emotional. Especially when there might be times when you are frustrated and potentially angry. Those emotions are negative and will be counter productive to an environment where you can improve the situation. Help those around you (and yourself) by staying cool and keeping things in perspective.

Chill the hell out.

You need to know *how* to relax and you need to **do** it.

Just saying 'Chill the hell out' is pretty loose advice. But you should look at it as advice that is designed to emphasise two things

1. Being able to relax and unwind is important to allow you to take an opportunity to refresh yourself and to recharge your batteries. But you need to know *how* to relax. Try different

things and evaluate the effect that each has. Try travelling, hobbies, exercise, group activities or taking time with your family. Get creative if necessary, but find what works for you to feel refreshed.
2. It's not enough to know how to relax. That is only half the battle. If you push yourself constantly you will break. Make the effort to **take the time** and decompress.

Your team needs to see you calm. If you're frustrated, discuss it with a confidante in private.

It's okay to be frustrated by something, but if you need to express that frustration, do it in private with a trusted colleague. Your team will take their cues from you.

The key message here is that you are always leading by example. Your team will reflect your actions and reactions for better or worse. If you want your team to be calm and confident, you will need to be calm and confident. This doesn't mean that you need to completely suppress your feelings and emotions. It's natural to feel frustrated when things aren't going your way. But if you need to blow off some steam or express your dissatisfaction in a cathartic way do it as privately as possible. Having a friend or trusted colleague who can sympathise is useful. And it's not necessarily a bad thing if your team occasionally hears that something has pissed you off. Just don't exhibit that emotion in public.

When you feel yourself start to lose your composure, stop, take a breath, relax, then speak politely.

Be aware of those times when your sense of calm is eroding. When you feel that things might be less than ideal, make the effort to detach from the situation and regain a composed state.

It's not possible to stay calm 100% of the time. You will be tested and therefore you need to be prepared to recognise when you might be reacting to a situation in a way that does not project the assured, in-control qualities of a leader. It's part of a process of self-reflection. This will allow you to take an objective view of your behaviour to ensure that it is appropriate. Fair warning, it won't come naturally. The best way to practise is to try to carry out an action that requires a calm approach immediately after strenuous exercise. You need to recognise that your natural reactions to continue emotionally can be controlled and therefore your outward appearance will be of someone that is in control. It's important that you recognise a movement away from calm early as it is easier to correct sooner in the process than later.

Suppress your sense of alarm in emergencies. Being calm helps everybody.

In times of crisis it is important that your team has an example that they can follow that will help them to deal with stressful events and demonstrate an infectious serenity.

Crises are times that test everybody. They present unusual challenges that people would typically not want to face. A natural reaction to pressure is to become more agitated and generally to look nervous and uncertain. As a leader in an emergency your job is to make sure that your team is able to function effectively to resolve the problems they are facing. By demonstrating a calm exterior, those around you will reflect your attitude and remain confident and in control. You should also be aware that by consciously working to remain calm, it will also directly help you to think more clearly and avoid a more emotional response that could be counterproductive. It's not easy to be self aware of your mental state in these types of conditions so the more time you spend considering your actions and reactions while times are peaceful the better your reaction will be in a crisis.

Be Inspiring

Being inspiring means acting in such a way to uplift and encourage others to improve themselves.

A team should always be able to look to a leader to get their cues for personal and professional standards of behaviour. This should be a conscious decision for any leader to try and motivate their team by displaying qualities that they want to be emulated.

Providing inspiration as a leader sets the standards on how to act and it also provides a vehicle for personal development of team members so that they can identify areas for improvement. Any opportunity to provide guidance and direction is valuable and as a leader this has the double advantage of letting your team know what 'good' looks like and helping them become better by example. The onus will always be on you to ensure that you are consistent and maintain a high standard, but the payback is a team that will be able to hold you in high regard and work to emulate you.

Don't demonstrate what can be done, show what's possible.

Encourage the growth and development of your team by fostering their capabilities, not by asking them to do something specific.

People are naturally curious. From that curiosity there is opportunity to extend from what is known and understood to discover things that are new and advantageous. As a leader you should be encouraging that curiosity in your staff so that they feel empowered to deliver results that are the product of autonomy and devolved responsibility. Give your team the authority to explore the opportunities in their work that can lead to new discoveries. Allow them to complete their tasks by solving problems in new ways. Make sure that they understand the boundaries that allow the organisation to function effectively (financial, moral, legal) and provide them with the support to develop themselves, their skill set and the organisation. Stay in touch with what is happening so that you can fulfil your responsibilities for good governance and support, but provide them with opportunities.

You are always representing your organization.

When the outside world looks at you and your team they see a reflection of your wider organisation. This impression will be favourable if you are efficient, organised, neat and professional.

It is easy to believe that your actions during business hours are the impression that people will have of you and your organisation. On the face of it this is true. However, if the way that you act at work is at odds with how you behave out of hours, then you can expect to be found out at some point. The easiest way to ensure that you will always putting on the best show is to **always** put on the best show. The more consistently you behave in the manner that best reflects an ideal standard, the more likely you are to actually live up to the standard. So act as if you are always putting your best foot forward and this will become your default state over time. This is a valuable life lesson for self improvement and development.

The team looks to you for how to behave. Set the tone.

A leader's standards are the standards that the team should aspire to. Set a consistently high benchmark in all things and your team will aim to emulate your example.

The very base definition of leading is to show the way. This is what you and your actions will do for the rest of your team. You should always be aware that you will be demonstrating the standard for what is acceptable for your team. Even without explicitly stating it, your behaviour will be the yardstick that they will use to measure themselves. This is a considerable responsibility and one that demands a constant vigilance to maintain. You will never find yourself in the position where you can encourage someone to measure up to a standard if you haven't demonstrated it. Where you see a member of your team exceeding your standards, highlight this and encourage it to be sustained.

Become a symbol of stability for your team.

People naturally feel more secure in the knowledge that there is a consistent reference point on which they can base aspects of their lives. You can become that reference point for your team that they can rely on.

Having a solid figure in a team that can be relied upon for consistency and relevance is an important role that allows team members to feel safe and secure. In a world where change and uncertainty are regarded as the norm, there are advantages to having a symbol of permanence that can be used as a reference. Be careful to appreciate that this doesn't mean that you should be adverse to change. You need to embrace opportunities for improvement and development and in the process, lead your team in driving for the advantages that change can bring. But along the way you need to epitomise the sense of stability that reassures people and helps them form a reference point from which to expand and explore.

A leader's role is to inspire the team's desire to complete their work.

The ideal team member isn't doing their job because they *have* to, they're doing it because they *want* to. Their leader's role is to help them to want to do their job.

You could look at this advice in a couple of different ways. Encouraging people to want to do their job might sound like a form of brainwashing. Forcing them to think in a way that is contrary to their actual wishes. The alternative (and the version that makes more sense) is that when people can see a value and purpose in their work they are more likely to be engaged. This helps them become enthusiastic and ultimately want to carry it out. It is easy to dislike being asked to do something. But believing that what you are doing is a good thing, either for yourself or for others, is rewarding and motivating. Set goals. Encourage a view of the bigger picture. Make sure that the context of what is being achieved is useful. Make a sincere effort at helping improve the conditions in which people are employed. These small things can help promote happiness and productivity.

Set standards for quality.

In the same way that a leader is responsible for the standard of the work that their team produces, they are also the person who sets the standards for the behaviours of the team.

Your team will take their cues from you as to the expected standards of quality and behaviour. Quality can be set by the work that you do and the instructions that you provide. Always be aware that your work and actions are an example for others. Review your team's work and make sure that your standards are being maintained. Demonstrate where necessary and correct where required. Don't compromise the quality of your own work for the sake of expediency or cost. This will be counter-productive as it will trickle down the chain of command to the rest of the team.

Your team should become used to an environment where excellence is the norm.

High standards are maintained by persistence and desire. Having a culture that promotes and supports improvement allows excellence to be a constant goal.

Achieving excellence in any particular task should be a realistic goal. But the greater goal should be achieving excellence in all things. This can only be accomplished by growing a culture in your team that desires a high standard and internally self regulates. This will be associated with pride in their work and the work of the team. As a leader you will need to provide the support to allow them to reach that level and once there, maintain that support in a visible way that encourages its continuance. The key is that the team should *want* to maintain a high standard as a **group**.

Leadership is influence.

Positions of leadership provide the opportunity to steer the narrative that is a team's work in a specific direction. A leader has control of the destiny of their team and themselves.

One of the most tangible advantages of leading a team is to be able to take an idea and make it a reality. As a leader you have a significant effect on the type of work that your team carries out and the *way* that they carry it out. You will be looked to for guidance and as an expert on process. In many cases you may not have control over the strategic application of your team's skills, but you can direct the manner in which those skills are applied so that they can be done efficiently. When you speak, people will listen. A suggestion will carry weight and praise is meaningful. This is a huge responsibility that needs to be carefully understood to ensure that you can manage and properly direct the efforts of those around you.

Everyone should have a hero.

Identify people who demonstrate the qualities that you want to emulate and work to improve yourself by following their example.

Learning by example is a great way to pick up positive traits and habits. As a leader you should take the opportunity to find someone who displays a characteristic that you want to display and make a conscious effort to emulate that behaviour. You don't need to tell them what you're doing (unless it starts to look creepy), just observe how they behave and try to live up to their example. You don't need to have only one hero. Feel free to pick several so that you can try to mirror different aspects of ideal behaviour. Think of it as stealthy mentoring. Sometimes getting the right mentor is difficult, but not if they don't know. Also be prepared to be a hero for others.

Leadership is not demonstrated in words but in attitude and actions.

If you need to tell people that you are leading them you should probably re-evaluate how effective you are being.

Leaders do. You should expect to be constantly demonstrating your ability to guide, encourage, empower and achieve. By doing this you are reinforcing your position as a leader so that others can follow your lead and work towards common goals. Don't try too hard to demonstrate authority and certainly don't enforce it unless absolutely necessary. Maintain a constant display of high standards and competency. This, more than words will tell people who is best placed to help them achieve their goals.

Leadership is about getting your team to do something you need done because they want to do it.

You will want to develop a culture in your team where work is enjoyable and actively sought.

Not all work can be enjoyable all the time. Finding the right motivation so that the act of *doing* the work because it is desirable, will be challenging. As a leader you should consider options that allow your team to develop satisfaction from supporting factors. Such as;

- The environment that they're in
- The people that they work with
- The feedback they receive
- The recognition that they get
- The autonomy they have
- The training required
- The challenges they have to overcome and
- The karma that they gain

There are plenty of different ways to spice up different tasks. You will find that just making the effort to improve the conditions associated with your team's work will have a positive effect.

You don't have to hold a position of authority to be a leader.

Leadership is being able to guide others to a goal. This could be because you have the expertise, or even just the inclination to help.

People won't *want* to follow you just because you are in a position of authority. And just to be clear, when we say '*want*' we're talking about a desire to follow your guidance, rather than wanting to stay employed. You should be inspiring people to accept your advice and follow your path because you have sound reasoning, a good plan and have explained what's going to happen so that everyone has bought into the ideas that you're promoting. That can all happen *without* being in a position of authority. To be honest, having a leader in a position of authority is just a good way to clarify their role and to provide a reference point for the team. Any degree of actual authority won't make you a better leader, it just provides a useful structure for the team.

Motivation

Motivating people is about encouraging them to do something

A team may require motivation to carry out a task or they may need to be encouraged to do something in a particular way. In the ideal world, a team will be galvanised to action because of their intrinsic motivators, but this may only be the case after being developed by extrinsic motivation from their leader.

Not everyone will be keen to progress a task in a particular way or to your timetable. A leader will need to be able to instil a sense of motivation in their team members that allows them to develop their own internal desires for action. Motivating your team can take two forms. The first is making sure that they are enthused about their immediate tasks and the second takes a wider view and should involve instilling motivation to carry out their work in general. This second form is the most effective trait since it allows the team to 'self-propel' through their work. For a team leader it involves instilling a sense of purpose in the work and pride and satisfaction in having carried it out. Once this is complete a team should be able to manage their own motivation.

Failure is opportunity for learning. Embrace it and improve.

Every goal that is not achieved is an opportunity to examine what has happened and to learn. Take this opportunity so that something positive can come from the event and next time success will be easier.

It's unoriginal to claim that failure can be a good thing. But if we examine the process of failure, it's obvious that the best response is to accept the fact of it with good grace and to get something useful back. First of all prepare yourself for failure. It will eventually happen. You will have no option other than to accept that at some point, you will not succeed. When it does you will have three obvious options.

1. Mope about the situation and generally appear as if you deserved to fail
2. Ignore what has happened and essentially absolve yourself of responsibility for the event
3. Realise that the only good thing that can be extracted from the process is the ability to learn and improve.

A leader will choose option 3.

If you develop a positive reputation, people will pay attention to you by default.

Being associated with a positive trait will lead people to associate you with other positive traits. As a result they will view the things you do and say with a degree of credibility.

A reputation for doing things well and generally being a good person will build a positive impression. This is an important asset for providing people with confidence in your abilities. It will only come about as a result of hard work and persistence. Once achieved, people will associate your past work and good deeds with future successes. This will mean that they will listen to your advice and pay attention to your activities. You will have an influence that will allow you to shape your environment and to direct people and activities. Do not underrate the importance of this facility. Realise that it takes a long time to build a good reputation but it can be undone quickly with poor choices. Once gained you need to protect it by maintaining it.

People work for you because they believe in you. Access to their talent is a privilege.

It's important to remember that the act of leadership is as much about repaying the faith of your team as achieving your goals. Respect their skills and give thanks that you have the responsibility of helping them grow.

Faith and belief are strong motivators for people and you should take every opportunity to develop and repay those feelings in your team. They need to know that you have their back, that you will defend them and protect them whenever needed. You will always be looking after their best interests and are always available to help them as individuals or as a unit. This is *your* talent. This is the thing that will make them want to respond in kind and make *their* talent available to use to carry out the work that the team needs to do. Don't take their expertise for granted and realise that when they are using it to help the team they are doing it because they believe in you. It's your responsibility to repay that faith with any and all the support you can.

Restlessness

Being restless is the trait of not being satisfied with the status quo and to constantly seek out new adventures and opportunities.

A leader shouldn't rest on their laurels. They should be searching for ways to improve and to push the limits of what is known. This can mean the acceptance of a degree of risk, but in a way that is designed to challenge the accepted norms and advance our understanding.

Change is an accepted fact of life. Without the constant evolution of our way of doing things we become stagnant and lose relevance. As a leader you should be looking for opportunities to 'mix things up' a little so that we challenge our preconceptions and look for new ways of doing things. This is something of a risky approach, so you will need to identify the risks involved and evaluate the situation for the projected benefits. Ultimately there will be occasions where you don't get it right, so you need to accept that there will be times that you find yourself needing to explain your actions. This is part of acceptance of responsibility and one of the reasons that you make sure to evaluate any such venture carefully. Don't let the risk of getting into trouble put you off. Evaluate, mitigate and initiate.

Don't be too cautious. Gather experience by getting into trouble occasionally

Risk is the way that we grow. Appreciate it and evaluate it, but don't be afraid to take it. Make an effort to stay out of trouble but learn from the experience when you find yourself in it.

As a leader you will find yourself needing to take risks. If you don't find yourself in these situations you may want to re-examine what your role is. Your job is to be able to evaluate situations and to determine a path forward. Risk and reward are typically related. High risk will go with high reward. Consider your options. Consider the implications of your actions. Seek advice from trusted sources. Accept that if you get into trouble as a result of your decisions you need to own the consequences and use the experience to become a more interesting person. Are you being told to take risks and to get into trouble? No. But when you *do* get into trouble, take the opportunity to learn from the experience.

Collaborative

Collaboration is about two or more people working together on a common endeavour.

Working collaboratively as a team is a force multiplier that allows different people and hence different approaches to tasks, to cooperate in solving problems and carry out projects.

As a leader you will need to promote and enable collaborative working so that it becomes a default standard for day to day business. While individuals can generally carry out tasks without problem, being able to work as a team means that different viewpoints can be combined to allow them to expand their perspectives. This is a key factor in tasks that require innovative thinking or for troubleshooting problems. Encourage cooperative thinking by providing good communication tools, promoting its benefits and by making time for people to use the process and see its strengths.

Get your experts together, tell them the problem, then back off.

A team comprises a considerable body of experience and talent. As a single unit they contain enough wherewithal to accomplish their goals. They will succeed by having the autonomy to do what's required and the space to get on with the job.

Teamwork is about using the strengths of different people to achieve a goal. Leading a team is about making sure that the right expertise is gathered together and that the problem is well articulated. Unless you are the only person with the subject matter expertise required to solve the problem, stand aside so that your team can get to work. Succeeding at their goal isn't just about being able to complete a task. It's about being able to do so with as little input or guidance as possible from you. The more independent they can be the easier your job gets. Help if required or asked, but letting them use their skills is exactly what they're employed to do. *Your* job is to make sure that they have the opportunity to do it.

Self Awareness

Being self aware is the trait of understanding your own personality, character, motives and feelings.

As a leader you need to be able to understand how your team members work and how to help them use their particular personality types to their advantage in their work. As well as that you need to be able to objectively understand your own personality type to be able to recognise what your strengths are and how to correct your weaknesses.

Self awareness is an incredibly valuable tool that will allow you to view yourself from the outside. The key is to get to a point of objectivity so that you can evaluate your actions and motives independently and correct or enhance as required. This will not always be easy and sometimes it might be a bit uncomfortable to face up to flaws that require correction. But the end result is a clarity of understanding about yourself that is quite liberating and which will greatly help you improve personally so that you can assist your team to improve.

Don't let feelings involved in a situation control the outcome

Often situations arise where there is an emotional component to the cause or solution. Trying to resolve these situations in a logical, dispassionate way can be difficult because people's perspectives will be skewed to different priorities. It's important to realise when this is happening and to adjust accordingly.

Emotional responses to situations are extremely common. This can range from decisions made when purchasing goods to emergency situations requiring urgent action. The best approach to mitigating an emotional response is to realise that it is occurring in the first place. A large part of achieving this is to work on your self awareness and to encourage it in others. Try to remove the personal investment in any situation. Work to make decisions more objective using lists of pros and cons or engage a different person to act as a peer reviewer. If you feel that objectivity has been compromised or that a conflict of interest is present you may need to consider changing the decision maker.

Past success does not guarantee future success. Guard against complacency.

Being successful in the past means that you have been able to demonstrate the ability to succeed. This is never an indication that you will be successful in the future. On the contrary, you might relax your standards on the assumption that you will be successful and this relaxation of standards will cause failure.

Being successful is a great thing. The more successful you are the better the chances that you know what you're doing. This is excellent. However, there is a very real possibility that you will become a victim of believing your own press, in the sense that if you don't fail you won't believe that you *can* fail. This form of hubris is obviously a dangerous thing and to some extent I have exaggerated it. The reality is that you will probably relax a bit every time you succeed and ultimately that lowering of standards will reduce your chances of future success. Be aware of the possibility of complacency and guard against it.

Constantly re-evaluate your own behaviour.

Behaviour evolves with time. A reaction to a particular situation in one instance will not be the same as any other. To ensure that appropriate actions are being taken use a self-evaluation process that is designed to make sure that the teams evolution is in a positive direction.

People change. They change with age, after training, following significant personal experiences or any range of influences. This process of change can be a positive outcome for improvement, but at the same time it could be detrimental. Set yourself development goals and benchmarks for personal improvement. Use these to evaluate your progress.

You don't need to solve hard problems alone. Admit when you need help.

Difficult problems require talent and hard work to resolve. Sometimes those problems are so large that they need more resources than are available. Realise when this is happening and get assistance.

This piece of advice falls under the 'recognise your limits' and 'don't be afraid to ask for help' categories. Often people in positions of responsibility resist seeking help for different reasons. They may mistakenly think of it as a sign of weakness or failure but the reality is that the only failure when struggling with a difficult problem is when you don't ask for help. Ask for help and do it often. Sometimes seek assistance even when you don't need it so that you can give members of your team experience.

Don't mock anything. Realise that you don't know as much as you think.

Making fun of things is a risky venture. It might seem like a good idea at the time to have a laugh at someone's expense but the reality is that if you mock something and you're ultimately wrong for doing it, you double down on the embarrassment at your own expense.

Mocking things is cheap. You need to be above that sort of thing. It's either a sign of weakness to poke fun at those who could benefit from your help or it's a sign of ineptitude when you mock something when you have no cause to. If you're not smart enough to understand that the act is poor form then you *certainly* don't know as much as you think.

Everyone makes mistakes. Including you.

People in a position of leadership are expected to display a high level of competence. In spite of an intention to get things right, it needs to be anticipated that sometimes things will go wrong. Leaders make mistakes.

It's unreasonable to expect that you will never make mistakes. You're in a leadership position so you will know that you are fallible. What you need to do is to make your peace with the mistakes that you make and accept them for what they are. Prepare for them mentally and move on from them by learning from each experience.

If you become cocky through repeated success, recognize that it's happening and stop it.

With repeated success there is a risk of complacency and overconfidence. This could lead to failure or to causing annoyance to your colleagues. Being *aware* that this can happen, helps prevent it from occurring.

Being cocky about your success or ability is simply setting yourself up for a fall. There will come a time when you will fail. If that occurs after declaring how good you are, it will be an unnecessary blow to your self esteem. It's unnecessary *and* undignified. Avoid self promotion and opt for humility. You can still feel good about yourself without proclaiming it in a boastful way. If you find yourself being overly full of yourself, dial it back. If you really are that good you shouldn't need to crow about it.

Look after your health. Preventative maintenance is better than emergency surgery.

Keeping yourself healthy is important. It's easy to neglect regular medical checks by imaging that you're saving time and that everything is fine. This is short term thinking based on the fallacy that you know as much about your health as a medical professional.

Looking after yourself should be your primary concern. You can't care for your family or your team if you get sick. Being proactive about your health is professional and responsible. Take the time to keep fit and well. At the same time encourage your team to do the same. Set a good example. Schedule a check-up in your calendar. You need to identify any problems early on and to minimize any downtime.

When you go to sleep, think about your successes, not your failures.

Staying positive is an important aspect in enjoying your work and staying healthy. When you need to relax you will find it easier when thinking about things that have gone well.

No amount of advice on trying to encourage positive thinking will completely help you relax. But part of being aware of the need to look after yourself is being realistic about how best to try. In this case remember that relaxing and sleeping is critical to staying healthy. It's common for high functioning people to worry about things that aren't going as well as they can. This is normal. What you need to do is to realise that thinking this way is normal, but that it is also not going to help you rest. Instead, force yourself to go over things that have gone well. Look at why you have had successes and the reasons that positive outcomes have been achieved. It's also alright to realise that it's an artificial construct to help you sleep. Knowing that it's a 'trick' doesn't mean that it won't work for you.

Everyone's a critic, but that doesn't mean that they're wrong.

Everyone will have an opinion on how best to carry out a task. This makes it easy to consider dissent as a normal approach to an idea that is sound. However, stay aware that there is very little difference between a good idea that has detractors and a bad idea that has detractors. Accept critical advice as a genuine concern for review.

You're never going to get it right all the time. The advice you should seek on different aspects of work will naturally contain a great deal of opinion that will differ from your own. This is healthy and provides opportunity for improvement. However, it can be easy to consider differing opinions as 'background noise' that while useful for the purposes of comparison don't necessarily add to functional improvement. Actively work to move yourself out of this mindset. Work to try to better understand the reasoning behind different ideas. Take an alternative view and approach the problem using a different context. Aim for complete impartiality in considering approaches to tasks. Your ideas are only *one* approach.

Recognize when you're being hypocritical.

A leader should actively avoid the appearance of hypocrisy and guard against inadvertently displaying it. Sometimes this can occur without being aware of it. Care needs to be taken to evaluate personal behaviour against required standards for the team and others.

Claiming to hold yourself to a particular standard when that isn't the case is folly bordering on fraud. Doing it in full knowledge that you're doing it is crossing a line that you should never breach. That said, there can be times when it's not obvious that you're not following your own direction and it will be detrimental to the morale of your team and your reputation for this to continue. Look for indicators that something is awry. Unusual questions from your team or requests for clarification on standards. You should be running a constant hygiene check on your standards and how well they are being realised, both for your team and for yourself. Take a critical view of your own behaviour and constantly aim to exceed your own expectations.

Positivity

Being positive is the act of anticipating that good things will happen.

A leader should be optimistic about any situation working out for the best. In the same way that a self fulfilling prophesy comes true because you say it will, acting positive has the effect of increasing the odds of a good outcome.

It could be argued that accentuating the positive is just a way of avoiding the possibility of a bad outcome. But this ignores the effect that acting as if things will work out well has on those around you. Despair and negativity feed on themselves. The more you focus on the bad things that could happen the more likely they will be to occur. A positive outlook will raise morale and encourage working towards success. The more you believe in yourself and your team the greater the odds are that you will win.

Get excited about your work. Enthusiasm is contagious.

Enthusiasm is a trait that people will observe and pay attention to. If you make sure that your enthusiasm for your job is obvious, others will take notice and reflect the same behaviour.

You should always aim to be employed in a role that allows you to enjoy what you do. You will always be more successful in a venture that you have a passion and enthusiasm for. Part of that success should be displayed openly as excitement for whatever you're doing. When people are having a good time, it's natural for those around them to feel positive and energised. This is a useful tool to influence your team and to help them enjoy their role as well.

There are insurmountable problems and extraordinary challenges. It's all a matter of perspective.

A leader's approach to problems will influence their ability to deal with them. A defeatist attitude will automatically put them into a mindset where they will accept and anticipate failure. Positively influence the chances of success by staying positive and regarding problems as challenges.

The simplistic semantics of calling insurmountable problems extraordinary challenges should not detract from the very real benefit that comes from maintaining a positive outlook and approaching times of difficulty in a manner that allows you to maximise your chances of success. You aren't trying to fool yourself or be unrealistic, sometimes shit happens and you need to deal with failure. But while you have any influence on the outcome you should always try to aim for success. Even bad situations can have positive benefits and you should be actively trying to maximise them. At the very least you will be able to demonstrate a positive attitude that should help your team to do their best.

When all hope seems lost remember that it's not over till it's over.

While the odds of may shorten, if there's still a mathematical chance of success, there's still a chance to prevail. Keep going.

If you're watching a sports event and the outcome seems foregone, always imagine under what circumstances the game could be turned around. If the score in a football game is 5 - 0 with 10 minutes to run, what would need to happen for the lower scoring team to win? Well, if they scored better than a goal every two minutes, they could do it. The chances are low, but there's always a possibility! You shouldn't give up for the same reason that you should carry a spare tyre in your car. You can't predict the future. As a leader you are expected to inspire and demonstrate a higher standard. One of the traits that should be at the forefront is that you will never give up. Never.

Invent new policy as needed. No-one will know.

When a new direction needs to be promulgated it's acceptable to put something together locally. Any effort is infinitely better than none at all.

Policy can be a word that will invoke an inner gag reflex in many people. All too often there is an association between bureaucracy and paperwork that seems to culminate in policy. Don't be fooled! Policy is your opportunity to set a standard for a process or activity that conforms to the way that *you* want it to occur. Think about that for a moment. Instead of being at the mercy of a policy that doesn't fit your requirements, you get to **set** the policy. It's not hard. Find a sample of a previous policy statement and plagiarise it. Don't be worried that you might not have it formatted perfectly or that it might not be right in the first draft. Anything will be better than nothing and encourage those who see ways to improve it to submit changes. Policy isn't hard to write, it's just hard to **start**. While we're thinking in this space don't regard existing policy as set in stone. If you want to change it, write something down and submit it to the responsible person with suitable justification. You don't need to rewrite it in its entirety. Just do the bits you want. If it doesn't get promulgated immediately, don't worry, simply having a change accepted gives you a degree of tacit approval.

Assuredness

Being assured is to be confident in your abilities, sure of yourself and your place in the world.

A leader should always project an impression of calm confidence. It should be this trait that others will look for so that they in turn can rest assured that things are going according to plan. In many cases leadership is as much about sending the right message as it is about making sure that work is carried out. A team should look at their leader and see someone certain of what they are doing.

Being sure of yourself in a leadership role means that you're going to have to get comfortable in your own skin. Accept the role and let it envelop you. People (external stakeholders and team members) need to deal with someone that is self assured and self aware. Guard against overconfidence and especially avoid arrogance. Put measures in place to have someone as a mentor or confidant that can act as an independent trip-wire to let you know if you are heading off piste. Be confident in your abilities and your position and act accordingly.

Don't concern yourself with what people think about you. You need to be your own person.

Self confidence will assist with perseverance in the face of criticism. Everyone is different. Every individual has their own way of doing things which is effective for them.

You are not in a leadership position by accident. You have been believed in and granted responsibility because you have demonstrated that you can do the job. Everyone is welcome to their own opinions on how things can be done. Ultimately the person whose opinion matters most is the one with the responsibility for carrying out a task. That's you by the way. You are the product of your upbringing and personal development. You will have a way of doing things that are your own. Other people will have other ways. Do things the way that **you** feel are the best.

Disciplined

Being disciplined is having the self control to to consistently follow a set of rules or standards.

As a leader, being disciplined is about demonstrating standards of behaviour and actions that can be relied on.

Being disciplined is advantageous whether you're in a leadership position or not. However, as a leader you have the ability to encourage your team to be more disciplined by demonstrating the practice. Set your standards and follow them. Be overt about what you're doing. Document what your expectations are for yourself and others. Call yourself out if you fail to meet your expectations. Take public measures to improve. A sense of consistency can be a comfort to others. It provides a reference point that they can rely on. Make that consistent behaviour positive and visible and your team will work to emulate it.

Social media is a time waster. Avoid it.

Communication is a cornerstone for effective leadership and teamwork. Don't confuse the kind of puerile assertions of "I'm alive. You're alive" for meaningful exchanges. At the best most social media platforms are exercises in wasting your time. At the worst they are intrusive hawkers of advertising that actively work to gather and sell your personal details.

Exactly defining social media is a problem in itself. In an environment of wikis, blogs, instant messaging and streaming information it would be a braver person than myself to say that any one platform was good or bad. There will always be opportunity for misuse. However, on the whole, wikis are effective repositories of information that will serve as constant, 'live' documents for reference purposes. Blogs act as a good way to capture historical information. They can also be used as a social exercise, so their mileage may vary depending on the individual. Instant messaging can be a quick means of communication, but it can also be intrusive and undisciplined and over-use can be worrisome. Platforms that combine multiple media types with advertising and the opportunity to 'like' or 'friend' others are typically towards the time-wasting end of the scale. Don't engage in it unless absolutely necessary and when you do, limit your use and exposure. Recognise it for what it is, a deliberate attempt to lure people into their ecosystem and to have their time and attention sold to advertisers.

Quality is not an action, it is a consistent pressure.

Being known for and carrying out quality work is something that comes with time and effort. Individual jobs can be of high quality, but there is only an expectation of that when it has been repeated many times.

Communicate your standard for quality to your team. This is something that they should ensure that they meet and maintain. Reinforce that meeting this standard is not something that they need to do when asked. This should be the minimum that is *always* met. Like any achievement that requires improvement, once it has been attained and sustained, it will become the norm.

Perfection is aspirational, but by chasing perfection we can attain excellence.

Aiming for a high standard will allow you and your team to achieve great things. Be honest with yourselves in thinking that the goal is aspirational, but still work to try and achieve it.

It's a meaningful exercise to aim for a state of perfection. The effort is noble and along the way you will approach things differently.

This will help you learn about the process and the thing that you are trying to achieve. Stretch yourself out of the comfort zone. Aspire to a state of enlightenment that is an ideal. This type of action will help you and your team grow. Recognise it for what it is. An opportunity to explore and experiment with a process to improve. Achieving that nirvana isn't the only way to win. Learning something new, improving in some way, raising a quality standard, these are all measures of success.

Aspire

To aspire to something is to aim to achieve a goal or ambition.

In the context of leadership, aspiring to something is about pushing your boundaries, to be a better person and to use that as an example for others. It's about desiring a higher standard and working towards it.

As a leader you shouldn't be comfortable with stagnation or mediocrity. Goals and ambitions allow you to push out of your comfort zone to achieve better things. Learn new skills. Set higher standards. Improve working conditions. Encourage your team to be ambitious. Look for opportunities to explore new ways of doing things that advance the common perception. Team members that feel like they're growing and developing will want to get better at what they do. By showing that *you* want to evolve and improve, your team will understand that this is the standard expected of them.

Don't just be yourself. Remember your best day. Be that person again.

Aim to overachieve. Constantly try to perform to the highest standard.

It's possible to get through life by simply going through the motions and letting the clock run out. No part of that will help you develop or provide a good example for your team. Always strive to do your best. Just the act of wanting to be better will help raise the bar on whatever you're doing. Honestly, anything else is wasting your time. If every time you do something you try to set a new standard, pretty soon the act of setting a high standard is the new normal. This will help you develop and improve and will act as a catalyst for your team members.

Exhibit the qualities of a leader that *you* would follow.

When trying to imagine how to display the best qualities of leadership, it's a useful exercise to consider what the qualities would be of an *ideal* leader.

As weird as it might sound coming from a book about leadership, the process of describing how to be a better leader is a difficult thing. A far better way to illustrate the right qualities is to imagine someone that *you* would follow. The reasons for this are not immediately obvious, but when you think about it, there is a sound logic to the process. Everyone is different and everyone would lead in a different way. Some would find the exercise a natural activity and some would never feel comfortable with it. But in general, the qualities of a leader that people will follow are universal and easy to identify (but somewhat harder to put into practise). Look at the list of traits outlined in this book and ask yourself if someone who displayed those traits would be someone that you would follow.

Leadership takes people on a journey. Sometimes to places no one has been before.

Accepting and providing leadership are activities that will have a lasting impact on all the people involved in the process.

Leadership is a calling for some and a goal for others. Whatever the reason that you are involved as a leader these things will be true.

1. It will take time and effort to build and maintain the qualities of a leader.
2. You will grow and develop as an individual.
3. Your efforts will build and develop those you lead.
4. The end result will be new and different.

Approach

The 'Approach' characteristic covers ways of dealing with a leadership role and the responsibilities that come with it.

It covers traits such as persistence, focus, commitment, flexibility and decisiveness. This characteristic is less about the work that you're going to do and more about the way that you're going to *do* the work.

This characteristic is difficult. It's about keeping your eye on the ball and making sure that the way that you go about your job allows you to be as effective as possible. You can't be a successful leader without demonstrating these traits to a high level.

The approaches that we will examine are;

- Persistence
- Resilience
- Passion
- Focus
- Decisiveness
- Commitment
- Patience
- Consistency
- Courage
- Confidence
- Realism
- Flexibility

Persistence

Persistence is the trait of continuing to pursue an objective in spite of difficulties that you encounter.

Persistence in leadership is both a personal trait that should be encouraged and a cultural trait that should be imbued in a team. No matter the endeavour, there should be an expectation that there will be problems of one form or another that will test the resolve of those trying to achieve it. Persistence is the force that will encourage people to overcome difficulties to achieve their goals.

Being persistent, encouraging persistence and demonstrating it to your team are incredibly important aspects of leadership. One of the few certainties of working to solve problems is that there will be difficulties along the way. The ability to persevere against adversity to achieve a goal is a trait that demonstrates strength of character. Others will seek to emulate it. Knowing and acknowledging the need for persistence beforehand is important. Expect it and recognise it when it occurs. Realising that you're fighting against adversity can often be a strong motivator. Maintain consistency. Don't fall into the trap of encouraging a dogmatic approach where a goal must always be gained just because you started down a path. There still needs to be a cycle of review to ensure that relevance is maintained. Stopping a task that is no longer relevant is not giving up. It's the product of a rational evaluative process.

Problems will always present themselves. Prepare, but don't be paralysed.

Problems will always feature in projects and general work. Preparing for them is sensible but don't let that preparation consume so much of your time and resources that you don't get work done.

Dealing with problems is part and parcel of the duties of a leader. You will be called upon to resolve disputes, correct deviations and prioritise conflicts regularly. Preparing for these eventualities is good practice as it allows you to deal with them quickly and efficiently when they occur. However it is important to remember that the list of things that could possibly go wrong is endless. Therefore you should realise that there will never be an end to preparing for problems. Do due diligence, evaluate the risks associated with your activities and put in place the appropriate mitigations. But remember that you will never finish a job if you never start it.

Succeeding, even at the very last second is still succeeding.

Remember that the measure of success for completing a job on time is not being ahead of schedule it's meeting a deadline.

Schedules are often set ambitiously with more of an eye to hope than practicality. In such a situation you will feel pressure to meet a deadline that may seem difficult to achieve. Be aware of the time constraints that you and your team are working under and adjust plans accordingly to meet your goals. This may seem daunting but continue to persevere. Being able to meet your goal even by a small margin is still a win that you can be proud of.

Resilience

Resilience is the ability to recover from setbacks.

Resilience is important for a leader and a team as it gives both the ability to adapt in the face of a loss or adverse outcome and to get back to normal operation. Being resilient is not an unusual trait in individuals, but each *team* dynamic is unique and requires close attention to ensure that it is maintained.

Being able to recover after facing adversity is challenging in any situation. Whether it be technical failure, tragedy, trauma, or stress. As a leader you need to be alert to the signs of problems that could occur, but you also need to be aware of ones that have occurred that you might not have had a chance to mitigate against (personal loss, serious health problems or similar). Once you have identified the need for recovery, that doesn't mean that you have to step in. People are naturally accustomed to difficulty and adapting as a result. However, the support element should never be overlooked and just knowing that there are opportunities for help can often be a positive influence on people. Being able to understand the process for recovery is useful and you should assist your team to recognise the thoughts and actions associated with recovery and to develop them wherever possible.

Make mistakes and learn from them.

Uncertainty is risk and risk invites the possibility of failure and mistakes. Accept that they will happen and put measures in place so that when they do you can make them learning opportunities.

People will often roll their eyes at the adages that *'failure is a learning opportunity'* or that *'the only way you learn is by making mistakes'*. They are often looked upon as excuses for failure or as a mechanism to put a positive spin on having made a mistake. That should not be the default belief and it is far better to have a plan for mistakes ready for when they occur, than to be left looking surprised when they do. Accept and expect mistakes to happen. When they do, have your team prepared with a plan for triage, mitigation and review that will allow the opportunity to become one that can be learnt from. Firstly make sure that the mistake is contained and reduce the impact on other work as much as possible. Then decide how to carry out the work that you were trying to do in the first place. During these processes you should be capturing information for a review of what went wrong and how it can be avoided in the future. This shouldn't take the form of an 'appoint blame' exercise and it needn't be lengthy or a burden on resources. Just find out what happened, document the way to avoid it in the future and let the relevant people know.

Passion

Being passionate is the trait of wanting to do something because you are internally motivated rather than for external drivers such as a salary.

We could consider passion for something as being a step up from enthusiasm. We can be enthusiastic about what we do and how we do it, but passion is driven from an internal desire. As an example, a person could carry out a task enthusiastically when asked, but if they had a passion for the work, they wouldn't need to be asked.

As a leader you should be alert to people with passion for different tasks for two reasons. The first is where that passion fits exactly into the needs of the team or the work being carried out. If this is the case, ensure that they can get the correct guidance and resources to move forward. The second occasion is where someone has a passion for something that doesn't fit into what they are trying to achieve. In this case, help to guide their focus so that they stay on track. People who are passionate about something will typically have an ability to concentrate in great detail on other things, since they have cultivated the skill in the area of their passion.

Passion is a poor regulator, but a powerful driver.

Being excited about something is a fantastic way to get it done, but be cautious of making judgements based on emotion rather than logic.

As a leader of a team and even as an individual you will realise that one of the best ways to get traction on a topic is to have enthusiasm for it. A person with a passion for something is more likely to work harder to achieve success than someone to whom it is merely a job. Select those who will enjoy a task above those who will simply carry it out. At the same time you will want to ensure that in the process of working in this area there needs to be a degree of oversight that allows for pacing progress appropriately and making sure that the direction is consistent. Keep encouraging progress and pay attention to how it is being achieved.

Focus

Being focused is the ability to concentrate intently on a task.

The ability to focus on an activity is incredibly useful for people, as distraction and the subsequent context switching that occurs is a source of inefficiency and a massive time waster. As a leader you should use focus to efficiently prioritise tasks so that you can get work done.

Being able to focus effectively is a highly underrated ability. It could be argued that in some roles (computer programming for example) the removal of distraction allowing complete focus is a major enabler to efficiency and productivity. Be aware of what your team needs to get its jobs done. Some will be more susceptible to distraction than others and some will require encouragement to stay on task more than others. As a leader you also need to make sure that you avoid flitting between tasks, and focus on getting achievements completed. Set the example for concentrating on one thing at a time and prioritise appropriately.

Do one thing at a time.

Allow your attention to be focussed on a single task to improve speed of completion and quality of work.

There is plenty written about multi-tasking vs single-tasking, and the buzz normally centres around increasing attention to detail and getting more done in less time. There will be arguments both ways, but it's worth taking a common sense approach and realising that if you were able to devote all your attention on a single task, the assumption is that you would be able to complete it in relatively quick order and you would probably be able to do a better job by having an opportunity to think the job through or to focus on the quality of the work. There are limits to how multi or single task focused you can get, but either way you won't be working any less busily. It makes sense to try and minimise distractions and in doing so you should be able to concentrate on the task at hand a lot better. Eliminating multi-tasking might be a bit of a stretch for most of us, but minimising it wherever possible seems like a good idea.

Get your own work done. Others will take your lead.

Be able to demonstrate that by getting on and getting work done, others will follow suit.

The problem being described here is when members of your team may have fallen behind on what they were supposed to deliver and / or they may be distracted by other work. Resist the urge to step in to assist them or to do the work yourself (it will be tempting). Instead, demonstrate that by persisting with your own work you can move forward and get stuff done. You may well have to encourage them onto the right path and don't be afraid to highlight the means by which they can move forward. But don't do their work for them. They won't learn and your time needs to be spent helping them to be able to do something, rather than doing it because it's easier in the short term.

If it feels like you're running out of time, start cancelling meetings.

Meetings have the potential to be time wasters. If you don't have enough time to complete your work, you don't have time to attend meetings.

Running successful meetings is something of an art-form. All too often they can wander off topic and lose focus. Always be wary of meetings that are unproductive. If you find that you are short of time you will need to seriously consider what your priority will be if you have a meeting scheduled. Here are some guidelines to consider when thinking about where your time will be best spent.

- *Can* you miss it?
- Meetings increase work. Not the opposite.
- Always send an apology

Once a decision has been made, don't second guess it. Focus on your next move.

Your role as a leader is to continuously move your team forward in pursuit of their objective. When you make a decision you are moving forward. Looking backwards and worrying about whether or not you should have taken an alternative is counter-productive.

The world is full of people who have perfect 20/20 hindsight and who will be happy to let you know what your alternative option should have been. While this '*advice*' can be given constructively, more often than not it will be done to make the advice giver feel superior. Don't fall into the trap of a) believing them to be wise or b) taking them too seriously. Self criticism is not going to help you move forward. Instead focus your energy on evaluating what your next steps will be. Use your energy productively.

Never regret a decision. It was the right thing to do at the time.

A decision is only ever right at the time that it is made. Changing situations will always provide different options so be comfortable with the decisions you make and move forward.

Decisions don't always go according to plan. Sometimes you might consider that an alternative would have been better. **Stop worrying about it.** Your job is to make decisions and to follow them through.

You should be able to make good decisions more often than not. Beating yourself up that a different solution might have been better is nothing more than a waste of energy when you could be doing something productive. When you made the decision it was made with all the information and forethought available at the time. You can't go back and you can't change the circumstances. Move on.

Clarity allows focus.

The more clearly you are able to see a problem or situation, the better you will be able to focus on dealing with it effectively.

The world is a chaotic place. Distractions and sensory overload are the norm. To be able to give your full attention to something you need to be able to remove distractions and allow yourself an opportunity to only focus on what's important. Remove clutter. Reduce background noise. Simplify.

Gain a reputation for completing projects.

You need to be able to finish what you start and to be someone who people will have faith in to complete work.

All too often projects can drift in scope and time. This can be for a wide range of reasons. However, whatever the reason it represents a failure of an agreement and ultimately a loss of confidence in those responsible for different aspects of delivery. Ensure that your involvement in projects is clearly defined. Be realistic about your estimates for completion and communicate progress to your customers often and openly. It's all about being able to set a target and meeting it. Use a specific fixed target as a milestone. Then meet the next one. Realise that your reputation for completion is as important as the completion itself since it provides confidence for your customers and your team.

Decisiveness

Being decisive is having the ability to commit to a decision.

In the context of leadership, being decisive is a vital trait. It could be argued that it's one of the **most** valuable. Recognising that a decision needs to be made, evaluating the options and committing to the decision are key functions of any leader.

If you're going to be a leader, you're going to need to know how to make a decision. Making decisions is a big deal. There are a large number of considerations that must be taken into account when making a decision, but that's not the same as committing to actually *make* the decision. A lot of people will endlessly work through evaluations. Some will vacillate between decisions. Some will just wait too long in a given circumstance. Make a decision while you have time and with the due diligence.

Your first impulse will often be wrong, but you have to start somewhere.

Don't let a fear of failure prevent you from getting underway. Think of the process as iterative rather than linear.

When you first start thinking about a project or task you will be acting with a bare minimum of information. This means that any initial considerations on solutions will not have the benefit of a complete understanding of the problem or the environment. The expectation should be that you will make decisions that will not be 100% correct. That's normal. What you should be able to do is to make a decision that will move you in the right direction. Use what you learn from the process to feedback and revise your thoughts. This iterative process will get you started and eventually have you focussed in the right area.

Decide.

A leader's job is to **make** decisions. **Make** them.

One of the responsibilities of leadership is that you are required to make decisions. This is not an easy task as it is the point at which speculation about options becomes a commitment to action. Just to be clear, your job is to **make** decisions. Not to vacillate about options or to constantly review risks. Do due diligence, but **make** the decision. People will typically *want* to be able to make decisions, but they won't want to take responsibility for the risks that they initiate. That's where the difference between a leader and member of the team becomes clear. A leader makes decisions responsibly and owns them, complete with the responsibilities that they bring.

You don't need consensus to make a decision.

Being a leader involves taking responsibility for evaluating and deciding on actions to take. The decision making process is about using the best information and your judgement. It is not a vote.

Leadership is almost always invested in an individual. That individual's responsibility is to make decisions. Those decisions are the result of gathering information, weighing the pros and cons and establishing what should be the best solution. The best solution will not always be the one that the majority of people think is best. Everyone doesn't have to agree before action is taken. The final arbiter of any decision making process is the person who holds the responsibility. Team members can (and should) provide arguments in support of options, but the leader will weigh these for likely success and decide on the course of action.

Making a decision is about choosing alternative options, not a choice between right and wrong.

Don't over-think a decision and blow it out of proportion. Keep a sense of perspective about the process and don't let it prevent you from selecting an option.

It can sometimes be easy to find a discussion about what decision to make, devolving into a situation where options are being over-simplified and represented as good or bad. This kind of polarisation is seldom the *actual* case and in practice, different options are just variations of degrees of better or worse. Be aware of falling into this trap yourself. It can generally be characterised by a discussion becoming less objective and more emotional. Avoid extremes wherever possible. This type of behaviour can sometimes be symptomatic of avoiding a particular option or trying to avoid making the decision at all.

The right option at the wrong time is as bad as the wrong option at the right time.

Decisions are actions that depend entirely on context. They need to be made at the right time for the right reasons.

Timing is everything right? At least in the realm of decision making it's a big deal. Making decisions effectively includes being able to make them and implement them in a timely manner. That doesn't mean as soon as possible, that means at the right time. Prioritise and schedule appropriately. Make sure that the cart doesn't go before the horse and don't prevaricate about a decision so as to delay it. By the same token, don't be forced into implementing a bad decision just because you're running out of time. Explore your options and look for alternatives. Either different options or time frames.

Make a decision while you have time.

As the time remaining to make a decision runs out so do your range of options.

Time is not your friend. You will never have enough and you will always wish that you had more. You have limited time to make decisions. As you spend more time considering your options the amount of time left starts to limit those options. Be aware of the time frame that you have to work with and always remain conscious of the amount of time available to implement your decisions. When in doubt it is preferable to decide early so that you have an opportunity to bank extra time for further consideration.

Don't choose based on who is right. Choose what is right.

When deciding, people are often swayed by an argument put forward by a convincing person. Always judge an idea on its own merits, not by the person who proposes it.

Any potential solution should be evaluated with consideration to the relevant factors. These should be as objective as possible and based on logic and empirical evidence. The means by which the information is established should be as neutral to the argument as possible. People will naturally bring an emotional context to a solution that will colour their thinking. This is true of people making an argument and of those considering a decision. Always try to understand the emotional subtext in discussions and try to compensate accordingly.

Realise that you cannot know that any decision you make is correct. So make it and move on.

Making a decision is an evaluative process the outcome of which can only be established by actually *making* the decision. Make it and move forward.

One of the great burdens of leadership is the acceptance of responsibility and the risks that must be taken as part of that role. There are no certainties involved in making decisions as a leader. The best that you can do is to minimise the risks wherever possible and eliminate some if you're lucky. You are in a leadership position because you are trusted to do the best you can. Realise that when you make a decision you are doing so with the right intentions and the best information available. *Not* making a decision would be a failure.

Consciously not making a decision is a decision not to take action.

Consciously not making a decision does not make you less responsible for the outcome. Quite the opposite.

Not deciding because you can't or won't make your mind up is an example of not fulfilling your role. *Actively* not making a decision is a choice that will have an impact that you should be expecting. It's perfectly acceptable not to decide if that's the correct course of action, but if you do avoid a decision you have accepted responsibility for that action. Whatever you do, don't delay a decision until you don't have time to make one. That is failing to do your job.

Any decision is better than indecision.

Having control of a situation involves interacting with it. Even a subtle influence on an outcome is a positive thing.

Even if you make a decision which doesn't ultimately solve a problem, at the very least you will have *tried* to improve the situation. Learn more by trying things. Take the initiative to influence how a situation is unfolding. Not being *able* to decide is a failure. It relinquishes control and leaves you open to outside forces. To have some influence over the outcome you need to have a degree of control.

Few decisions have all the information needed for a certain outcome.

Decisions are seldom straightforward. They will involve research, consultation and ultimately a degree of intuition and incumbent risk. Can a result be guaranteed? No.

Making decisions are exercises in acceptance of risk. If the process was straightforward and repeatable a machine would be doing it. We start the process of coming to a decision by accumulating as much information as possible to support an outcome. There are a myriad of ways of collecting information, but ultimately there will come a point where the data stops and you will need to step in. It might be time that forces your hand or it might be the funding to continue research. Whatever the cause, at some point you will need to apply the good judgement that you cultivate to determine a result. That's why humans still make decisions. It gets to a point where you need to take a leap of faith or accept the path of least apparent risk.

Make a decision before your problem changes.

Problems evolve as the environment evolves. As time passes by, the options for solving a problem change and so does the problem.

Problems are dynamic. As time passes they change. The same is true for the solutions and the decisions that need to be made to enable them. This tells us that you have a limited amount of time to establish the details of the problem that you're trying to solve. Bear in mind that you will be required to make decisions quickly but you will also be asked to make the *right* decisions. Sometimes you will need to take a leap of faith to make a decision before the situation changes. Not doing so can lead to a constantly changing problem that you will never be bold enough to try and solve.

Leadership involves making decisions. You either make them or you default on your responsibility.

One of the jobs that you accept as a leader is to make decisions. This is a responsibility that you agree to and others rely on you to carry out. Not doing so is a breach of faith.

When you move into a leadership position you should do so with the full knowledge that the role involves the acceptance of responsibilities that some other people will have difficulty with. One of the more significant of these is the responsibility to make decisions. It's your job. People expect you to do it and they trust that you will do it in a responsible way to the best of your ability. Don't look to others to make decisions for you. Don't avoid them and don't make them without due diligence. A great many people covet the opportunity to have control of a decision making process, but fewer want to accept the responsibility that it comes with. It's yours.

A good plan enthusiastically started straight away is better than a perfect plan started next week.

Always opt for taking the initiative when taking action. Doing so allows you time to review, re-evaluate and refine your direction

There are a range of sayings that encourage the 'starting early' option ("The early bird catches the worm", "First in, first served") and they're there for a reason. Being able to get started on something early allows a direct advantage in being able to gain experience or allow for time to evaluate options while working towards your goal. Of all the resources that you can have at your disposal, you can't buy or manufacture more time. The only other option is to utilise it wisely. Starting a project early gives you options. Not just for the job at hand, but for the follow on work that can also benefit from starting early.

A reputation is not built on what you are going to do.

People who have achieved things are respected. Once someone has achieved something they have proven themselves.

Building a positive reputation involves an effort in demonstrating capability. This requires time and persistence, working to achieve a goal and then doing it again. No matter how many times someone describes how they *would* do something, that is no substitute for having done it. Be the person who does things.

Leadership is actioning priorities. Management is making sure that they're carried out.

Leadership and management are different skills. They require different approaches but don't forget that they are working towards the same result.

The best way to think of the difference between leading and managing is to consider the process of completing a task. A manager will ensure that the right resources in terms of people and materials are available. A leader will make sure that the team tasked with doing the work are clear in their direction and focused on the task to completion. Both roles can be combined in the same person but the skills required are different. Neither is more important than the other but neither can exist without the other.

Refusing to decide is the worst decision you can make.

One of the main leadership functions is to make decisions. Refusing to do that will not solve the problem you are facing and it is a broader failure in leadership.

To intentionally refuse to make a decision would be an extraordinary thing. The only situation under which it would be acceptable is where not making a decision *is* your decision. However, what we're talking about here is when someone *refuses* to make a decision. There are reasons why it would happen, but unfortunately they are all indicators of someone who is failing in a leadership role. That is unlikely to be what the person *wants* to do, but it would most likely be an indicator that they realise that they are unsuitable for the job.

Commitment

Being committed is accepting and completing a task or a process.

A leader needs to be able to get on with things. Committing to a task means seeing it through to the end and more importantly it also includes deciding on a course of action and getting underway. The alternative is vacillation, doubt and ultimately no progress.

As a leader you need to be someone that can move forward, stay the course and be relied on. Committing to an action or way of doing business should come as no surprise and might even seem obvious, but it's always easy to defer decisions or to sit on the fence when giving advice. If you're going to do something, do it and follow through with it. If you're asked for your opinion, give it. Avoid indecision.

Finish what you start.

An unfinished project is a liability against being able to complete future work. Starting something means planning to finish it.

We have probably all come across individuals who have great ideas and who are enthusiastic about jumping into working on them straight away. That's a really exciting way of approaching work, but we have probably all also come across people who habitually start jobs when they still have unfinished projects that still require completion. People who finish jobs get work done. People who just start jobs create work for everyone else. When you start a job have a clearly documented plan, schedule and finishing point. Follow the plan. Keep to the schedule. Reach for the finish point. **Then** move on to the next job.

It's OK to have an opinion on issues. In fact it may be compulsory.

Don't be afraid to have an opinion and to pass it on. Taking a leadership role means making decisions from the best information available. Opinions are a best guess. A leader is paid to do their best.

Some people will fear voicing their own opinion. Depending on the person or the opinion this may or may not be a good decision. However, as a leader you are responsible for being able to advance an idea or to ensure that action is taken when necessary. This means having to draw a conclusion or make your best guess at something so that you can move forward. You will need to draw on your experiences and intuition and consult as widely as practical, but ultimately you will *need* to form an opinion that is your own. Sitting on the fence on an issue can sometimes be a barrier to progress. Voice your opinion. Allow your thinking to be evaluated and challenged. You are a leader, your thoughts should be measured and considered. They are worth voicing and will be essential to making sure that you and your team can move forward.

Once you have decided on a direction and started work, commit to the action.

Being able to decide and move forward is an essential trait for a leader. That doesn't mean that you can't be flexible, but once you start a project you need to focus on completion.

When you start a project you are committing to following it through to an agreed milestone. More often than not this will be to completion. Any doubt or vacillation will be a cause of confusion and delays. This does not mean that you don't continue to evaluate progress and relevance. This needs to be an ongoing process to ensure that the project will meet its objectives. Even though you will remain open to the possibility of change, you must remain focused on moving forward in accordance with the plan.

Progress means getting started.

There is only so much thinking about a task that can be done before taking action to commit to it. Don't delay getting started through unnecessary doubts or worry.

It is very easy to become so concerned about potential problems with a task that you perpetually delay getting started. This shouldn't be confused with not doing due diligence and considering the risks appropriately. Herein lies the balance that a leader will be evaluating. Make sure that you stay aware of the potential for over thinking the problems associated with a project at the expense of getting under way. Consider all the appropriate factors, decide and move forward.

Patience

Patience is the trait of staying calm and waiting for the right opportunities.

A leader will need to practise the virtues of patience to ensure that they can make the right decisions at the right time. It is also the awareness when dealing with people that getting lines of communication established can take time.

Patience is more than a virtue for a leader. It is an absolute necessity. You will need to take your time to make sure that your customers, stakeholders and team members are fully informed and understand all aspects of ongoing work. This will almost always be difficult because of the differences between people. Your perseverance will sometimes be tested. You should anticipate and allow for explaining things in different ways depending on your audience. Make decisions by allowing yourself the time to get the right result. Don't rush things if you don't need to. Time is a tool that you can use to get a quality result.

In a new environment, be cautious of change until you understand what's happening.

When a leader is in a new area they will need time to get a feel for the environment and the personalities. They will need to make sure that they understand the follow-on effects properly before initiating any changes.

Starting in a new environment requires time to establish a good grounding in the people, resources and work requirements. During this time you are gathering the information that you will need to be able to understand the dynamics of the organisation and how they are interconnected. This is necessary so that you can appreciate the impact that changes in one area will have on another. Make sure that you don't carry preconceptions into a new role. Establish the facts for yourself and use that knowledge to decide on any changes you want to make. Sometimes there is an obvious need that will be the reason that you're in the position. Don't be afraid of making *necessary* changes, but use observation and research to ensure that you have the right appreciation of the situation before attempting them.

Decide quickly where there is a chance to review and slowly when you only have one shot.

Pace your decision making to suit the circumstances. Where you can develop a solution by iterating through different situations, use the opportunity. If you only have one chance to try a solution, take as much time as practical to maximise your chances of success.

Being able to make decisions quickly is advantageous because it allows time to iterate and change direction if required. That's not a good enough reason to make a quick decision. They should always be made in an appropriate way for the right reasons. However, if you have the opportunity, it is an advantageous option. If your decision can only be made once, you have to take your time to consider all the pros and cons. This will maximise your chances of getting the best outcome.

Try your best to help people understand, even when it seems unlikely.

As a leader, your best resource is always the people around you. Helping your team, customers or any stakeholder understand what is going on will ultimately help you achieve your goals.

As a leader you need to be able to communicate effectively with people. That doesn't just mean your immediate team. It means that you must be able to transfer information in a manner that allows it to be understood to your customers, the stakeholders and the public in general. Build positive relationships to make the process easier. These are always an investment in success. Once people understand what you are trying to achieve, they have invested in it. Any degree of investment is beneficial since it allows them to support you in some way or even to identify something that you may have missed that will impact on the success of the work.

Consistency

Consistency is being able to carry out an action the same way or to the same standard multiple times.

A leader needs to be reliable and consistent. They should be a rock of stability in a sea of uncertainty. Their team should be able to use them as an example of how things should be done. Inconsistency breeds doubt and differing standards.

One of the things that make people feel comfortable is the sense of familiarity that comes from dealing with a dependable process, product or person. As a leader you should always aim to provide a consistent service. Look at the way that you carry out your business and the quality of the final product. Make sure that you pay attention to the details as well as the big picture. When you demonstrate consistency people will rely on you.

If you let the little things slide, everything slides.

When setting limits for things that are or aren't acceptable, the limits must be sensible and adhered to. If they aren't then there may as well not *be* any limits.

Setting rules and regulations should be approached with caution and an eye for a minimalist implementation. That should allow your team the flexibility to carry out their work in the most efficient manner possible. When it's necessary to set fixed limits they need to be clearly established with good reasoning. Once done they need to be enforced. A rule without consequences for avoiding isn't a rule. It's a guideline at best. If it's okay to break one rule it's okay to break others. Set the rule. Set the limits. Publicise. Enforce.

Courage

Courage is committing to a course of action that involves personal risk.

A leader can be expected to display courage on a regular basis. This is a direct result of the acceptance of responsibility that comes with the role. Courage will not necessarily involve heroic actions that will expose you to physical risk in the generally accepted definition of courage, but a leader will be expected to commit to decisions where the outcome is not certain.

A leader cannot be risk averse. It is a fundamental tenet that you will face decisions which can, and will, sometimes go wrong. Part of being a leader is realising and accepting that fact. It takes a degree of fortitude to face up to the challenges of leadership and that is at the heart of the role. Don't regard the trait as being gung-ho. Measure and evaluate your actions with due care and deliberation. The opportunity to display courage will come in many forms. It could be dealing with people and difficult situations, facing up to flawed practices or making tough decisions. Face each opportunity as a challenge to demonstrate your capability.

When catastrophe threatens, it's acceptable to try something risky.

Solutions with different levels of risk are appropriate for situations with different degrees of impact.

In times of crisis there is often a need to act decisively and at short notice. Likewise, when making a decision of a routine nature with little pressure on the outcome it is acceptable to consider your options and consult as required. The underlying message is that you need to be able to adapt your responses to changing situations and to have the courage to sometimes make decisions without as much due diligence as you would like. Rest assured that you have been placed in your role because people believed in you and your abilities. Don't be foolhardy, but don't be afraid.

Talk with your enemies. The results may surprise you.

It's important to ensure that you consider a wide range of options and opinions when making decisions. This should include seeking the advice of those who may think differently to you.

It's a truism that nobody gets along with everybody they meet. Often we find ourselves having significantly differing views with individuals that can manifest in poor relationships. This is always unfortunate, but it should be recognised as a simple fact of life. Equally true is the fact that it's impossible to know everything about everything. Be brave enough to approach those who you might not see eye to eye with so that you can consider a full range of possible alternatives. Maintain a courteous and professional approach (as you should always do) and you may discover ideas that you would never have considered and possibly find some unexpected common ground.

Results are more important than protocol.

Sometimes to achieve your goals it will be necessary to go against conventional ways of doing things.

Protocols are laid down to ensure that there are a consistent, efficient and reliable way to do something. It's important to note that this does *not* make it the right way to do something. Before you start down the road of making up the rules as you go along, recognise that protocol gets established for a reason, so it's not something to challenge lightly. But don't be afraid to throw a flawed system or procedure into the light so that it can be reviewed.

Also recognise that sometimes there are immutable reasons for things that transcend efficiency or practicality. A good example of this would be the law. Break the law and you're on your own. But think of the reasons for maintaining protocols as being a spectrum that goes something like: good idea - guidelines - best practice - policy - rules - law. Sometimes protocols are based on good ideas that have outlived their relevance. Don't be afraid to challenge them in the name of getting things done.

Getting your point across clearly is more important than following outdated protocol.

Being able to communicate clearly should be a priority if faced with the dilemma of whether or a convention should be followed.

When we talk about protocol here we're talking about social norms / rules of convenience or flat out bureaucracy. Don't go out of your way to challenge it. The goal here is to ensure that communications are clear and understood, not to be an iconoclast for the sake of it. Be aware of the risk of causing offence and judge your actions appropriately. Be creative about how you approach the issue and be aware of the personalities involved to try and anticipate their reactions for potential mitigation.

Some of your decisions will be mistakes. Realise that you have to make them anyway.

A leader has to make decisions. You will not be able to always make perfect decisions, so accept it and prepare appropriately.

Making decisions is one of the key functions of leadership. Not everyone's comfortable with the process, but **you** *need* to be. In a position of responsibility and as a leader you will sometimes be required to make decisions that will have a significant impact. As much as you can have confidence in your abilities, you also need to be aware that occasionally you will get it wrong. That cannot stop you from making decisions. It's a hard thing to realise that sometimes you're going to get things wrong, but it would be the height of hubris to think that you won't. Accept it and be courageous enough to do it anyway.

If you create enemies, don't shy away. They're just as afraid as you are.

If you find yourself having significantly differing views with individuals that have manifest in poor relationships, realise that they will be as concerned about it as you. Don't be afraid of being honest about your differences.

It's not possible to get along with everybody. This is always unfortunate, but it should be recognised as a simple fact of life. It's natural to have a degree of self-doubt about who might be in the right or wrong, but recognise that this will go both ways. Always maintain a courteous and professional approach (as you should always do) and wherever possible maintain a good dialogue. Don't project any negative emotions in communications and it's a good idea to restrict your personal opinion on them wherever possible. Not only is there a possibility of your feelings becoming known to them, but it also sends a message to the person in whom you have confided that you are struggling internally with the relationship.

Admitting your failures shows confidence and strength. It reassures others that failing is acceptable.

Being brave enough to describe your failures reinforces the positive aspects of learning from mistakes and encourages others to do the same.

No one likes to fail and fewer like to admit their failures, but as a leader you need to be able to set a standard that will promote the positive aspects of the process of failure.

It's important to emphasise and reinforce that;

- It promotes honesty and openness.
- There are learning opportunities in failure.
- Taking appropriate risks is a good thing.

Ensure that any failure is documented in a way that others can learn from it. If a similar event in the future is successful because of the lessons learned, make a point of highlighting it.

By leading the way in admitting areas for improvement you build a reputation for being someone that can learn, adapt and improve.

Ignore rules that make no sense.

People make mistakes and times change. When a rule is invalid because of a mistake or it's out of date, work around it.

This direction sounds a bit gung ho. But it's there for a reason and it falls under the 'Courageous' trait as the decision to go against what is laid down as a directive is not to be taken lightly. Often in the development of a business or organisation, a rule is developed that seems like a good idea for the time, but as time moves on its relevance diminishes. It's also possible for a rule to be generated by someone in error or in an area where they may not have fully understood its practical implementation. Ultimately this can result in a rule that no longer serves its purpose and for all intents makes no sense. It should be patently obvious that the rule is to be ignored.

When considering ignoring a rule ask yourself these questions;

- Is it a rule or a guideline?
- Is it written down anywhere (if it's not written down, it's not a rule).

With all of the advice given above, it's important to remember two things.

1. Firstly if you're going to ignore a rule because it does not make sense you also need to bring it to the attention of the appropriate people so that it can be amended. If you like, make the amendment and suggest the change.
2. Never assume that you're right in thinking that the rule is bogus. Get a second opinion from someone in case you're not seeing something obvious.

If you never fail, you're not extending yourself.

It's a function of leadership to take risks. To learn and develop you need to risk failure. If you've failed, it means that you've pushed the limits of what you're capable of and in the process learned something new.

You should not be afraid of taking risks as part of the leadership role and as a consequence of that you will be exploring new activities and ways of getting things done. Remember that this is not an option if you're a leader, it's an expectation. Pushing the envelope of what is considered normal is necessary to develop yourself and your team. At some point some of those risks won't work out. Learn from the experience and improve. Just remember, repeated failure is indistinguishable from incompetence.

Your orders do not dictate your courage. Your courage determines how you interpret your orders.

People cannot be directed to be brave or courageous. Instead they will display bravery in the way that they approach their work and in the wider sense, their life.

An act of courage is something that is associated with personal and / or professional risk. You won't attempt something that requires bravery because of the risk, you'll do it in *spite* of the risk. You will do it sometimes in opposition to your orders and often it will be an act of selflessness. It will be done because you believe it to be the *right* thing to do. The easy option is seldom the courageous one. Expect to be tested, but in the process you will be become a better leader and person.

Follow spirit of the rules first and their exact wording second.

Rules are written to enable consistency of action. When it appears that their intent has diverged from their words, it is most likely that the intent is the correct option.

Rules are written to provide specific boundaries to general expectations of what is the right thing to do. The more specific the rule, the less likely it is to be able to remain relevant over time. Be alert to inconsistencies in what is written and what is expected. In the perfect world you will be able to inform the relevant people of the problem, but if this isn't possible before needing to take action, you have a responsibility to bring it to their attention after the fact.

Remember that when the opportunity arises to make rules or policy, the more clarity you can provide to the intention of your words the better. It's always wise to leave the details to your team members.

As a leader you are burdened and blessed with the right to be wrong.

Leadership involves understanding the need to make decisions and having courage to do so knowing that failure could occur.

Making decisions is a hard thing for many people. The harder the decision and the greater the consequences or risk of failure, the more difficulty they will have. As a leader you will have a mission and an area of responsibility. Both of these should be clearly defined. If they aren't, you need to correct that. Within your area of responsibility you get to make decisions about how your team and your work progresses. You have significant influence and opportunity to carry out your tasks successfully. You also have the opportunity to mess things up badly if things go wrong. Your duty is to recognise and accept the responsibility and to make decisions knowing that sometimes they might *be* wrong. The good news is that a leader is allowed to be wrong sometimes. You can't make correct decisions 100% of the time.

Keep your fears to yourself, but demonstrate courage.

Leadership depends on appearances. Internal concern is acceptable, but outwardly there should be composure and no fear.

Emotions are one of the things that helps define us as human beings. As a leader you will be a model that others will follow. If you show concern, your team will be worried. If you project confidence those who follow you will be confident. Never underestimate the power of outward appearances. Always aim to demonstrate the emotional stability that will help your team achieve their goals. This doesn't mean that you have to be a automaton, it's okay to enjoy yourself. But when the chips are down, your team will follow your lead.

Anyone can lead when the times are good.

When the environment is benign it will always appear like an easy job to be in charge. The quality of a leader is shown when things go wrong.

There will be good times and bad times as a leader. In the good times you will wonder what the fuss is all about, but when problems arise you will be tested. Everyone will have detractors and those who believe that things should be done their way. It's good to have differing opinions to draw on for alternative ways of doing things. You can expect to encounter occasional resentment when you make decisions which not everyone agrees with. There may even be some indication that others would covet your authority. This is a natural reaction for people who see the leadership in the good times, dealing with day to day issues and providing guidance. It's also fair to say that they may be right. In times of calm, there will be many correct answers to problems and a team can move forward pretty smoothly irrespective of which particular option is chosen. However, when pressure is applied, crises arise and difficult choices need to be made. Often those who would wish some degree of leadership responsibility come to realise that the job is more than it may have appeared.

This doesn't mean you should discourage those who seek leadership roles. Quite the opposite. This should be encouraged, nurtured and developed. But one of the things to emphasise and demonstrate is that strong leadership comes to the fore when things are going badly.

Have the courage to say what everyone knows to be true but isn't saying.

Speaking an unspoken truth is a difficult proposition as it usually involves a topic that people have trouble facing. A leader needs to have the courage to explore difficult subjects.

The fable of the emperor without clothes is the most widely recognised example of this situation. In the fable it is only the innocence of the young that overcomes the fear that the wider population has of speaking the truth. This topic is really about having the courage to speak the truth and not to ignore difficult subjects. As a leader you need to set the example of facing up to the truth and accepting the risk of speaking out. This is your job. It can't be delegated.

Confidence

Confidence is an assurance that you are right and you have the capability to carry out a task.

A leader should be confident in their abilities. They should be able to draw on their training, experience or innate ability to carry out tasks or to make decisions. Confidence allows those you lead to have faith in your direction and to follow your instructions more easily.

Confidence is not a trait that can be trained. You will need to develop it over time with experience. Having said that, some people learn the skill at a young age and it carries over into their working years. Have faith that you are in a position of responsibility because those who selected you believe in your abilities. Your team will look to you for direction and will draw their own confidence from your demeanour. When making decisions, the process should be robust and appropriate to the circumstances. When you make the decision, be confident about the action. Avoid deliberate over-confidence. It exposes you to doubts about your abilities when decisions do not go the way you intend.

Back yourself. You have capability.

You are in a position of leadership because you have demonstrated an ability to carry out the requirements of the role. Trust that ability.

Often when starting out in a leadership role it can seem daunting. This comes with the realisation that there is a considerable amount of responsibility that you are assuming for your team and the completion of tasks. The first thing that you should accept is that this is normal. The second thing to realise is that you didn't get to the position you're in without having people recognise that you have the capability to cope with the situation. They have faith in you and your potential. Relax. Trust that you'll do fine. Confidence will help guide you to success.

Approximations in advance are more useful than certainty in hindsight.

Being able to provide an estimate of progress or some other metric is useful for others to help them with planning. Approximations aren't bad when appropriately qualified.

As a leader you should be able to make estimates and predictions against the tasks that you are working on. Not being able to do this is an indication that you are either not familiar with what is going on or that the work that you are responsible for is not going according to plan. Providing estimates is a function of your job. Another function is to make sure that those predictions are as accurate as possible and any uncertainties are articulated. Beware of over promising or underestimating required work. Always remember that it is better to under promise than to raise expectations without basis.

Make it appear as if you know what you're doing, even if you're just picking a colour.

Being a leader means inspiring confidence in others. So when you're making a decision, you want to be *seen* to make a decision.

This advice isn't about faking a skill or embellishing your abilities. It's about being confident and being seen to be decisive. That's not an attempt at boosting your profile as a great decision maker. It's about making sure that your team and customers are confident in the team and how it is achieving its goals. Big decisions will be made with the appropriate consideration for the task. Smaller decisions should get the appropriate attention, but the *same* commitment for action. If there are decisions that are appropriate to delegate, do so and oversee their implementation to make sure that the same commitment is being applied.

Stand out in a crowd. When there is a need, take control.

A leader needs to be visible and ready to take charge. Doing so should be a natural action.

By definition a leader should be someone that is set apart from the crowd in one way or the other. This is will most likely be by virtue of their approach to life or their actions, but irrespective of their natural skills they need to accept the responsibility for being the first person to step forward to tackle a problem or to accept responsibility. Believe it or not this is an easy thing to do. Simply volunteer for everything (assuming that you have the time), when faced with the option to try something new, accept immediately. Pretty soon the instinct to 'do stuff' will be normal. Encourage others to join in. Initiate 'doing stuff'.

Be flexible with rules and regulations. Hire smart people and trust in their judgement.

Clever people will be able to ensure that they can help achieve the goals of the team through applying themselves in an appropriate way. Being flexible with managing these people allows them the leeway that they need to achieve their goals.

Rules and regulations are important and provide the guidelines that are required to ensure that tasks are carried out in a safe and compliant manner. A leader should be confident enough in their team that they can allow them the flexibility to approach their work in a way that complies with the required guidelines and can get the job done. Smart people will have creative ways of working and achieving goals. Make sure that they understand the limitations they need to work under and let them get on with it.

Temper prolonged deliberations about decisions. Make them and move on.

Affording due diligence to decisions is appropriate. Just make sure that due diligence doesn't extend into over-thinking the problem and putting off action.

Making decisions is an important part of being a leader. Being able to make decisions in the *right way* will help define the type of leader you are. It's common when making decisions to try and remove as much risk as possible. This means careful consideration of your options and assessment of the way forward. This can become a problem when considering risks and potential hazards drive the project into stagnation before it even starts. You can't foresee every hazard or mitigate against every risk. At some point you need to decide if you can press on or call a halt. Being a leader means taking responsibility for acceptable risks. Consider your options and move on.

Doing things takes strength, but it requires more strength to decide *what* to do.

Accomplishing a task is a commendable feat, but accepting the responsibility for deciding to start a project and its direction are actions that require the acceptance of risk and the confidence to be able to complete the task.

In no way should the efforts of people working to complete tasks and carry out projects be minimised. This is hard work that demands dedication and professional work practices to achieve success. But this is a separate effort to the acceptance of responsibility required when deciding which tasks and projects to proceed with.

This responsibility extends beyond the task at hand and encompasses the organisation as a whole. Tasks and projects support the wider business and enable wider success or failure. Making the decision on which things to do must take into account appropriate processes and accept the risks that are presented. Deciding to accept these takes strength of character to move forward.

When placed in command, take charge. That's your job.

A leader isn't just expected to lead, they *need* to lead. Their authority should be unquestionable.

The act of taking charge of a group and moving them to accomplish a task demands a unifying force to provide a common drive and direction. When you take charge of a team you can't do it by halves. You need to be in control and you need to be *seen* to be in control. Take advice and seek feedback to help execute the task, but leave no doubt that **you** set the direction.

Think for yourself.

A leader needs to be able to draw information from those around them, but ultimately they need to make and justify decisions knowing that *they* are responsible for them.

Thinking critically about problems and solutions demands an ability that will mark a leader as a person with a relatively rare skill. That does not make them *special* or better than other members of the team but it does highlight a strength that they bring to the team. It makes sense that this skill is used to best effect by taking advantage of it. As a leader you strengthen your team by considering the options and evaluating progress. You can use all the assistance you need, but you should be confident that you are the right person to be carrying out the job.

Realism

Realism is accepting and acknowledging the *actual* state of any situation without bias.

Failing to acknowledge the real world as a leader will invite failure. To make effective decisions you need to know and act on the most accurate information possible. A leader should be able to gather input from as many sources as practical and evaluate them without putting their own slant on it.

Being realistic about a situation might sound somewhat obvious, but as a leader you will be tempted to bias your view of the world with your own pre-conceptions. That's because you are constantly being called upon to make decisions based on your intuition or to evaluate and make calls on less than a complete picture. It can be very easy to think that you can appreciate a situation without all the facts or go with your gut. Sometimes that might be true, but to fail to get a realistic overview of all the conditions you are working under is reducing your chances of success. Be honest with yourself and your team and accept the obvious.

Don't try to go at full speed all the time. You'll burn yourself or your team out.

Working hard all the time will end badly. You and your team need to balance urgency and intensity with decompression to make sure that everyone stays healthy.

Working hard is a good thing. It means getting things done and extending yourself and your team out of a comfort zone to grow and develop. However, a high pace sustained for too long will have a detrimental effect where the pressure to deliver will manifest itself as stress and ultimately failure. Recognise the signs of wear and tear on yourself and others so that you can balance a sustained effort with an opportunity to relax and breathe. Be open about needing to look after your team, and trust and encourage them to keep an objective eye on you.

Intuition is valuable, but it's no substitute for facts.

Intuition is a talent that is honed through experience and application. But always remember that decisions are at best highly educated guesses. They are more reliable when based on facts rather than instinct.

It would be wrong to evaluate intuition as either a magical insight or lucky guesses. There's a saying that goes something like "*The better you are, the luckier you get*". Essentially it's stating that you can make better decisions by being good at what you do. There isn't much mystery involved in being able to solve problems intuitively. Get experienced at what you do and ultimately the decisions you make will have the benefit of a wealth of knowledge. But no matter how good you get you must always remember that a fact will always beat a guess. Estimate or approximate if necessary, but always check the facts when you can.

Be realistic about your project timelines.

Providing accurate schedules for projects is as much about being honest with yourself as it is about being honest with your stakeholders.

There is a strong tendency for people to underestimate the amount of time that a task will take. Whatever the reason for this you will need to be aware that it happens and to be wary of doing it yourself. When you make an estimate of time required to complete a task you are not being asked to exaggerate your abilities or to be ambitious. You are being asked to help someone else align their schedule. The more accuracy you can provide, the better placed the receiver of the advice will be. Be honest with your estimates. Declare any concerns about progress or unexpected advances. Highlight risks that could impact the project and what their implications are. Keep your customers apprised of progress if your timetable changes.

Don't negotiate unreasonable schedules. Encourage honesty and realistic time estimates.

Your team and those who support you need to be able to carry out their work in a way that reflects a realistic expectation of the time required to carry out tasks. Make sure that they are not forced to try to meet unlikely or impossible schedules.

When scheduling tasks, there is a degree of uncertainty about time frames that is only to be expected. There is always the possibility that the work will go smoother than expected and there is also the possibility that the work will take longer. Take care when planning workloads and timings for tasks with your team. Do not approach it as an opportunity to try and force an artificially faster time from them than would be reasonable or practical. If the time frame cannot be met or if it can only be met by impacting on some other crucial body of work then it is better that a more accurate plan is forecast. This guidance is really about dealing with people in good faith. Don't deliberately expect more from people than they can deliver. This will only end in disappointment for all parties.

Flexibility

Flexibility is the ability to vary an approach or opinion.

A leader needs to be flexible to enable them to adapt to changing requirements and to meet challenges by trying new techniques without fear of failure.

Staying flexible means being able to change and vary your approach to problems to develop the best solution. If you can't adapt, you can't evolve. You need to be able to meet varying challenges by trying new approaches and rethinking established practices. Expect to change your perspective and to discover that you need to alter your direction. This should be default thinking when starting any body of work.

Always be ready to change direction.

Times change and situations change. A leader and their team need to be alert to the potential to change direction as requirements dictate.

It's an uncertain world. There are plenty of reasons why you and your team may need to alter what you're doing. You may discover that you're doing something the wrong way (it happens). The situation or context under which you're working could vary. The customers requirement might change. Whatever the reason, you need to stay alert to the possibility for change and when the *need* arises be willing to accept it. I have deliberately highlighted the word 'need' in the previous sentence, because one thing you *don't* want to do is to change without good reason.

- Recognise the need for change.
- Determine the new direction.
- Change.

Quickly recognise and correct bad decisions.

Cultivate the ability to objectively reflect on your decisions and when you become aware that you have made a bad one, correct it quickly.

Decision making processes are fallible. Leaders are required to make decisions at times where a lack of information or insight will increase the risk of getting something wrong. Accepting that it's going to happen is an important aspect of leadership. Equally important, but arguably more difficult is recognising that you have made a bad choice. This is hard. Often times it will be compounded by a reluctance to accept that it has happened. You need to be objective about positive or negative effects and to make sure that you correct them when required. More often than not the first indicator will be someone else bringing it to your attention. This is golden advice and use it wisely. It's either someone doing you a huge favour or an opportunity to help someone understand the situation. Either way, approach the advice in a neutral way and evaluate it on its own merits. If the decision you have made is bad, act accordingly and quickly.

Maintenance is just as important as new capabilities.

The operation of the systems and services that form your organisation represent the inherent value of your business. Don't neglect these while experimenting with new functions.

Chasing shiny new capabilities is an activity that is usually an attractive and enjoyable process for team members. The process of improvement is a vital part of development and growth that is to be encouraged. However it also needs to be recognised that such activities will naturally detract from 'business as usual' work and if this prevents your core business from functioning it is a bad thing. There is a resource overhead required for development that needs to be present in your group to ensure that normal operation is sustained. This means making sure that there is manpower available to carry out research while pursuing new capabilities, such that if maintenance is required on standard services it can be carried out without problem.

In an emergency, don't be afraid to relax protocol.

Protocol is there to ensure that the right thing is done at the right time. In an emergency there is a change in what is considered important and as a result some protocol can be considered irrelevant.

Emergency situations are simultaneously exciting and worrying. They will (hopefully) be rare occurrences that demand special attention and sometimes unique methods to resolve. Your team members will be focussed on resolving the problem and as a result will have prioritised steps to deal with the emergency above many other things. This means that expediency will often become a priority at the expense of niceties and convention. You need to accept it and focus on ensuring that the bigger picture is being taken care of. If possible, keep a track of areas where common protocols are dispensed with or relaxed. It's possible that they could be altered to take into account similar events in the future without compromising normal functions.

Progressive

Being progressive is to advocate change or improvement. To be enlightened and forward thinking.

Leadership involves adapting to change in a positive way. Not only should a leader be developing this skill in the people that work for them, but they need to be able to recognise the need for it in themselves.

Don't think of being progressive as being the same as being *a progressive*. It's more important to be able to be self aware about the need to review and adjust, than to be labelled as someone who desires change. This trait focusses on the requirement in a leader to be able to recognise the need for the need for change. That's not a typo. It's easy to identify that change is a positive thing, but less simple to understand that the act of requiring that need is important. Consider the future in a strategic way and develop methods to impart change that positively influences your team and drives the *desire* for change.

Pick your battles. Let some things go. REALLY let them go.

You only have a finite amount of time and resource to tackle problems. Decide which ones to focus on and put the others out of your mind.

There will always be more problems to face than opportunity to solve them. Realise it. Come to accept it and then do the hard part. The hard part? Not worrying about the things that you have decided to ignore. There will ALWAYS be injustices you can't correct. There will ALWAYS be people you can't help. There will ALWAYS be problems that you can't solve. You have to find a way of putting those thoughts aside so that you can concentrate on the things that you *can* correct, help and solve. Realise that worrying about one thing while you're trying to solve another will not help. Remind yourself that you only have *so* much time and resources. Concentrate all your energy on the problem directly in front of you.

Values

The 'Values' characteristic describes the principles that you need to display and adhere to as a leader.

It covers fundamental personal traits such as honesty, responsibility, humility and being selfless. This doesn't mean that you need to be a saint, but it will allow your team to believe you, and more importantly, to believe *in* you.

Be under no illusions here. Having the right values for the job is essential and they are the hardest thing to learn. These traits are at the core of a person and are typically formed at a young age. It's about being a good person and doing the right thing. Sometimes that means making hard moral choices and the guidance in this area should provide some thinking points.

The values that we will examine are;

- Honesty
- Acting Ethically
- Trustworthiness
- Transparency
- Accountability
- Responsibility
- Respect
- Humility
- Generosity
- Selflessness

Honesty

Honesty is the quality of speaking and acting as you indicate you will.

Behaving with honesty is a critical trait for a leader. Your ability to work with others will entirely depend on others trusting you. Having a reputation for honesty allows others to start working with you more easily.

Think about the immediate benefits of honesty by imagining having to work with someone who you don't trust. This is a characteristic that should not be taken for granted. Nurture and build your reputation for honesty. It takes time to develop but the advantages are clear. Always remember that honesty is difficult to prove but easy to lose. Don't compromise on maintaining it. Always reward honest actions in your team. Often honesty is the reason that you get delivered bad news. Deal with the downside of such a situation but appreciate the effort that went into bringing it forward.

Debate honestly. The goal is to arrive at the right conclusion, not *your* conclusion.

Discussions with your team and others is aimed at coming up with the best solutions to problems. Going into a debate with the intention of going in a specific direction is disingenuous.

You should be in a position of leadership because you're a clever person. That doesn't mean that you have a monopoly on the best ideas. Engage in talks with anyone who can add value to a discussion. Listen to what is being said and evaluate it objectively. Making a decision in advance of discussions is a shameful waste of everyone's time and should be beneath any respected leader. Your credibility is on the line if you go down this track and others will have difficulty trusting you in the future when you are found out.

Speak honestly, and encourage others to follow suit.

Be honest and open when communicating to enable clarity and make sure that the rest of your team does the same.

Speaking honestly describes a manner of speaking where people are encouraged to be open and frank (but civil) in getting their message across. All too often people tend to err on the side of caution or aim to protect some perceived sensibilities when talking. When done in a social sense it is an effort to make sure that people can get along, but when done for the purposes of business or trying to accomplish a task it hinders the message by adding a layer of abstraction that detracts from the 'real' information. Sometimes honesty can be 'uncomfortable'. One or both parties may not wish to confront a difficult issue or to bring a problem fully into the light. This is an illusion of convenience which simply avoids something important at the expense of clarity. Not only should you be willing to 'grasp the nettle' when discussing things, but members of your team should be encouraged and should feel comfortable raising difficult topics in an environment that values honesty.

Question authority, and permit others to question yours without fear of reprisals.

A leader should honestly evaluate information and irrespective of the source, be prepared to highlight concerns whenever they occur.

When we talk about questioning authority, we should ensure that we don't just think of it in terms of those in seniority, we need to include those in positions where their knowledge should make them a subject matter expert. We need to operate in an environment where each of us is comfortable in seeking clarity from anyone and where we are comfortable with anyone asking us to justify ourselves. This is seldom an easy thing. It stems from the fact that as a person in a position of responsibility (whether in a management hierarchy or in terms of expertise) it naturally follows that the decisions we make and the conclusions that we come to are expected to be the best possible. However, that understanding is mistaken. We are *all* fallible and whether we have made a mistake or whether a person asking for clarity is simply doing so because they are not as experienced, we owe it to the wider ideal of doing the best we can to accept outside enquiry and to constantly re-evaluate our decisions.

Don't aspire to external goals, aspire to live your life a certain way.

A goal is simply a stepping stone. It is more important to set and meet a standard for living. This will require applying yourself consistently to achieve a desirable way of life.

Setting and achieving goals can be a noble pursuit, but it doesn't necessarily speak to the quality of the person or the achievement. A longer term approach is to work towards a 'way of life' that allows you to be someone that you aspire to. For example, instead of thinking that you would like to receive the Nobel peace prize, you could aim to be selfless and honest. This is an approach that makes its own rewards and in many ways provides opportunities that come largely unseen. That doesn't mean that you simply drift through life aimlessly, but think of the process of achieving goals as a secondary effect of living your life a particular way.

Acting Ethically

Ethical behaviour is identified by people's concept of what is right or wrong.

A leader should always strive to behave in an ethical manner. Other's perception of your actions directly affects how they deal with you. Make sure that those perceptions are positive and reflect your ability to know right from wrong.

Doing the right thing is a by-product of knowing right from wrong. Always strive to ensure that you act appropriately and that you encourage the same in others. Act as a role model and hold yourself to a higher standard. Acting ethically is almost one of those situations where if you look after the little things, the big things follow naturally. Make a point about doing the right thing and use those actions to support the same behaviours in your team. Be aware that as a leader you will become an arbiter of right and wrong. Use those opportunities to reinforce a positive culture.

Sometimes you won't know the right thing to do, but you still have to *try* to do what's right.

Leaders face challenging decisions. Sometimes these involve evaluating the moral or ethical implications of actions (or inactions). There may be **no** good answer or the best option may be unknown. Irrespective, the decision must reflect the genuine effort to do the right thing.

You are going to occasionally be confronted with decisions that will only result in bad outcomes. You might need to determine the *least* bad outcome. You may face a moral question that requires compromising a belief or standard that you would rather not have to change. Prepare yourself, because they **will** happen. When they do, don't flinch from the task. Analyse, evaluate and determine the best way forward. Consult and take advice if possible and document the decision for posterity if you think that it will raise questions in the future. Whatever the case, the important takeaway is that you should ensure that in spite of the decision not being to your liking, you should always try to make it for the right reasons.

Rules do not cover every situation. Sometimes *you* will have to decide what is right.

Leaders cannot expect to be faced with decisions that are always clear cut. Their strength will be in the ability to make determinations in situations that no-one has foreseen. When they occur a leader will be expected to determine the correct course of action for the right reasons.

You will occasionally be called upon to decide what 'right' looks like. It might be an moral or ethical dilemma or a standard that needs setting. The situation will be new and unique. You will need to evaluate what the implications are for yourself, your team and the wider business. Based on what you determine you will make a decision that sets a precedent for those who will come after you. You get to decide what the right thing to do is. There is no real way to prepare other than accepting that the situation **will** happen and when it does, you will be required to act with the benefit of your experience and skills. Don't second guess yourself afterwards. Always remember that the decision you make is made with the best information available at the time and in the context of the situation.

Doing the right thing is better than doing things right.

Making decisions on the basis of ensuring that the right thing is done will be a facet of all leaders. Occasionally this will come at the expense of a standard or preferred way of doing business that will challenge the accepted norms.

You're going to have to make difficult decisions. Doing the right thing means working to an agreed plan to ensure that tasks are carried out by your team in the best way possible. Support the organization's mission and look after the team. There will inevitably be conflicts that mean you will need to choose between such things as business practices, standards, ethical and moral points of view and legal concerns (that list is far from exhaustive). **Always** aim to maintain the moral high ground in any tricky decision. You will need to look back on decisions and live with the knowledge that irrespective of the circumstances, you made a choice that was the *right* thing to do. In spite of the fact that you might need to justify yourself after the fact, you will want to do so with a clear conscience.

Trustworthiness

You are trustworthy when people can rely on you.

A leader has to be trusted by their team and their stakeholders. Trust promotes loyalty and engenders strong relationships. Not being trustworthy means failure as a leader.

You need to be trusted in order to have people believe in you and what you say. Take your time in building up trust relationships, they're important to you and everyone you interact with. Once established they need to be actively maintained and monitored. Time is a crucial factor in developing trust. It isn't created through a strictly logical process (I.e. if Bob says "you can trust me" this is not a suitable basis for that trait to be generated). It's a process of providing evidence that the things you do and say can be relied on so that after a period of time you can be taken at your word that something will happen and people will *believe* that it will happen. In this respect, trust can almost be viewed as an absence of reasons to distrust (which can be assumed to be a default setting).

If your team doesn't trust you, you are not a leader.

Team members of a successful group *want* to follow their leader. They will trust that the decisions being made and the direction they are going are correct.

A successful team will believe in their mission and the way it is being achieved. A leader will not always have the opportunity to completely articulate the reasons behind the details of the tactical and strategic decision making. But if their team trusts their leader they will have faith that the right decisions are being made for the right reasons. Without this trust a leader is reduced to constantly needing to justify their actions or needing to enforce the team's direction and progress. Trust enables efficiency and unified purpose while at the same time promoting engagement and confidence.

Keep confidences.

The hard currency of trust is quantified in the ability for a leader to do what they say. An important aspect of this is the ability to keep confidences.

When you are entrusted with information that should be limited in its distribution it is always important to remember that the need to limit its distribution is a by-product of ownership of that knowledge. Someone cares about protecting the information. That means that *you* need to care about protecting it to the same degree to maintain the confidence of the original owner. It's always good to remember that you should keep other's confidences the same way that you would have them keep yours.

Transparency

Transparency is a quality of openness and sharing that promotes knowledge growth and trust.

Transparency in a leader allows greater engagement in a team and with external stakeholders. Clarity of purpose and action grows trust and alignment towards common goals.

Transparency is an enabler in a leadership role that significantly aids trust and allows for better visibility of what is going on and more importantly *why* things are happening. In practical terms this is as small a thing as talking with your team about the decisions that are being made and how they affect the wider organisational goals. In a broader sense, being more open could encompass publication of plans and information that outlines strategic objectives that give wider context for actions. Trust and confidence grow from a 'no surprises' approach that transparency provides. This then encourages engagement and builds better relationships at different levels.

Transparency builds trust.

Being open and honest in your dealings with people will allow them to trust you.

Mistrust comes from uncertainty. Sometimes it comes from the sure knowledge that you *can't* trust someone. If you consistently deal with people in a way that allows them to see that what you say is your genuine intention they will believe what you say, even when they are unsure about a situation. This is a vital asset to a leader. Often you will need to be able to direct people to do things that they may not understand fully. In such a situation the natural response is to question the motive or instructions. But if the people you are leading trust you, they will be more likely to simply act on your direction and get the job done.

Accountability

Accountability is the practice of accepting responsibility.

A leader accepts responsibility for themselves and their wider team and goals. They are accountable for outcomes that they contribute to and work to ensure that there is a pathway for recognising and learning from those outcomes.

Being accountable is often associated with the phrase "The buck stops here" that was prominent on the desk of US President Harry S. Truman. By having this in place, President Truman accepted that **he** was accountable for his personal actions and those of his wider presidency. Ultimately, accountability is tied to responsibility in the sense that it should be a very singular attribute. As a leader you need to clearly identify and publicly acknowledge your role in making decisions and accepting their consequences. This has greater emphasis when things go badly than when they go well, but realise that this is an additional burden of your position. When things *do* go wrong, you should also have the responsibility of correcting the issue. Part of accountability is being the first responder for fixing problems. Avoid blaming any other element for failure. Acting as a victim of circumstance is counter-productive to putting things right. In this respect, being accountable means actively working to improve things.

When you make a mistake, apologize right away.

Nobody is infallible. Mistakes are an inevitable part of decision making and life in general. Correcting these as efficiently as possible requires that the problem is recognised and dealt with as speedily as possible. An apology is a good start to a process of correction that works to preserve relationships.

You're going to get things wrong. Everyone does. Reacting to these events is more of an indicator of character than when things are going well. One of the best tools you can employ as a leader are the relationships that you build with others. When you do end up making a mistake it is important that you act to preserve those relationships. A large part of the process is *recognising* that you have done something wrong. For whatever reason you might have missed it. Look for clues and react accordingly. A pre-emptive apology is a good way of setting the groundwork when you see something go sideways. You may or may not have been at fault, but apologise anyway. Ask for help to correct the problem and if it turns out that you're not at fault be gracious about it. Also make sure that you accept other's apologies for similar events. Recognise that the process is first and foremost about maintaining good relationships so that you can put things right.

Make decisions that are yours to make.

Making decisions are an important leadership function, as is knowing the scope of responsibility. Involvement in making decisions outside a specified role opens the organisation up to inefficiency and confusion.

You are going to make a lot of decisions as a leader. You will get so used to making decisions that you will find it dangerously easy to extend your activities further than your remit. Working in an organisation means being able to allocate resources appropriately and being able to manage those resources appropriately. There is a good chance that you will be a leader in an organisation where there are other leaders looking after other areas. Work hard to interface with other teams efficiently with clearly understood boundaries and responsibilities. Crossing into another unit's role opens up the very real opportunity for misunderstandings and confusion. Other units will operate with a corporate understanding of their role and will be able to make decisions with the benefit of a different context to the one that you will have. Respect that and realise that accomplishing the organisation's mission is a task that requires coordination and awareness.

You need to be able to make a decision and wear the consequences.

Decision making as a leader involves accepting responsibility for the outcomes. When things go well this is an easy process, but when things go badly it is important for a leader to assume responsibility and manage the outcome.

The consequences from decisions can vary widely on a spectrum. Success or failure is not a binary outcome and severity exists on a graduated scale from minor to significant. This is where being able to accept the responsibility for your decisions becomes more important. You should already have a good understanding of the potential impacts of any decision based on the consideration that you undertake when making it. This should prepare you for the range of eventualities. In a positive outcome make sure that you are comfortable with accepting appropriate responsibility, but ensure that you emphasise the work of the wider team. When a decision goes wrong, realise that it happens sometimes. You can't change events that have occurred, but you can mitigate their effects and work to correct things. Own the problem and put yourself in a position of responsibility to make things right.

Leadership takes responsibility. There may be reasons for failure, but never excuses.

A leader takes up an important role in a team. Coupled with the responsibility of overseeing the completion of tasks to carry out the organization's mission, a leader accepts responsibility for the success or failure of those tasks. When a task is not completed correctly a leader's focus is on mitigation and rectification, not assigning blame.

You will not be successful with every task you attempt. Your process for completing work should include at the very least a rudimentary risk analysis prior to starting so that you can evaluate potential areas where things could go wrong. When they do (and rest assured it will occasionally happen) establish the reason so that you can learn and improve. This should form a standard response in such situations. Active attempts to assign blame or make excuses is a failure in itself. If you and your team need to learn something new and make changes, it is imperative that you do. Making excuses for failure is time wasting and demeaning.

Responsibility

Being responsible is being accountable for your actions.

For a leader, responsibility is a commitment to be the person that will ensure that a thing happens or that something is done in the correct way. It's important to make the distinction between something happening and being the person that provides the *guarantee* that it will happen. Leadership is in a large part the act of accepting responsibility for your team and for their actions. *Being* responsible is about caring that your responsibilities are carried out.

As a leader you will have responsibilities and you need to *act* responsibly. These are two different but related things. Your responsibilities are to the organisation that you work for, the tasks that you are trying to achieve and the people that you are working with. Acting responsibly means facing up to difficult decisions, knowing your limits and doing the right thing (this list is not exhaustive). In a relatively crude sense, being responsible is acting like an adult. There are things that you need to do and ways that you need to do them. Accepting both of these and putting them into practice can sometimes be hard, but that's all part of growing up :-). As a leader, concentrate on looking after your team and providing a good example. Acting responsibly will serve as a standard for others to emulate.

As soon as you find out that someone in your group is definitely toxic, get rid of them.

A toxic person will have a seriously detrimental effect on a team. As this type of behaviour is part of the core values of a person, the best advice is to use the most effective method to get them off your team.

People who are described as 'toxic' can be thought of as suffering from a serious personality flaw that manifests as a problem that is obvious and which makes them highly unlikely to be redeemed. For example, someone who cannot be trusted because they have stolen from their workmates or compulsively lies would be in this category. But there are also more insidious forms of the behaviour where people will create divisions between team members for sport, deliberately work to undermine authority or bully others. Often these people will not be easy to dislodge as they will be otherwise very clever and possibly (outwardly) good at their jobs. The best advice is to seek guidance from peers and management to ensure that any and all occurrences of antisocial behaviour is well documented.

When communication is breaking down, you're responsible for trying to change the language.

In times where it seems as if different parties are not able to get a common understanding of each other's position, you need to be the person that recognises that a change is required and tries something different.

A fundamental aspect of good leadership and working effectively as a team is communication. But as communication is a process where two different parties need to have a common understanding or start point, sometimes there is a breakdown in that process that results in difficulty getting good information interchange working. This could be as a result of a range of problems such as experience levels, difference in approach, geographic separation, communication methods or even the **actual** language being used. Whatever the reason consider it **your** responsibility to recognise that a problem is occurring and find a way to correct it. Don't let the situation sit and fester. Be proactive and positive.

Do not give advice on matters you do not understand.

Giving advice is a serious responsibility. It is irresponsible to provide advice on a topic where your understanding is poor.

People will naturally feel a degree of pride at being asked to give advice on a topic. It is a sign of respect and of the regard that the requester has for a person that they would ask for advice on any matter. However, do not fall into the trap of providing information and advice on topics you do not fully understand. While it is tempting, you run a considerable reputational risk and you put the requester in a difficult position. It's important to remember that you are measured by the accuracy of your knowledge and advice. If you start distributing information and opinion in an area you don't understand you're risking the level of credence that any future advice you might give will have.

No one cares as much about your team as you do.

Leading a team means looking after them. If others offer to take care of some aspect of your team's needs **you** are still responsible for making sure that they are looked after.

Your team is your responsibility. Accepting that responsibility is a deeply individual thing. They will be your responsibility during work hours, at 2 a.m. and in the weekend. While you're on holiday they're still your responsibility. Someone may be asked to look after their needs temporarily but they won't care as much about them as you will. This is not a responsibility you can delegate while you're in the role. For that reason you should always keep in touch with what is going on and how the team is being looked after. If there is ever a problem with the team it is your responsibility to sort it out.

Take full responsibility for your team's mistakes.

Your team is yours to direct and develop. When your team fails you're responsible for the failure and the resolution.

As a leader you should consider your team as being the most important tool of your trade. The advantage is that this tool can be adapted and tuned to constantly improve and develop. Your role is to ensure that your team is prepared to meet the challenges it will face. If it fails to achieve what it sets out to do, the failure is yours. This is **your** responsibility. Failure is not the end of the world, just an opportunity to improve. Use it wisely and prepare your team its next challenge appropriately.

Always follow directions, except when the directions are wrong.

As a leader you need to follow the advice of experts and your own management. However, you need to apply critical thinking when evaluating those directions to ensure that they are correct and make rational decisions on how to proceed.

Responsibility is a blessing and a curse. A leader accepts that there is a need to act responsibly to achieve their goals. You'll be in receipt of considerable advice from those around you and direction from those who are tasking you. All of which needs to be evaluated for relevance, accuracy and priority. Establish trust relationships that will allow you to determine what weighting to apply to advice and determine good boundaries to ensure that your direction is appropriate. When faced with a situation where you are directed to do something that you believe to be wrong you are responsible for speaking up to make sure that the situation can be addressed and resolved. Ultimately remember that you need to maintain your integrity, so always be honest and open in dealing with the diverging needs and always stay true to your values.

Don't let upper management dismantle your team.

Your team is an extension of yourself. Those who would affect your team should do so with your advice and guidance.

A team and its leader are intrinsically meshed. It is not possible to duplicate a team or to copy and paste success. Often situations will arise where it is envisaged that a successful team can be duplicated by division and growth. This is a fallacy. A team is only as good as its leader and a leader is only as good as their team. A good team needs time to grow and develop. Trust and expertise must be grown over time and with the right nurturing and guidance. There is no shortcut to building a successful team but there *is* a shortcut to destroying one. Don't let people break your team apart in the interests of duplicating success. This is not possible. Let a new team grow with a balance of good leadership and recruiting. You should take any proposed (sensible) changes to your team personally. Because they **are** personal.

Fight for what you know is right and be prepared to recognise when you are wrong.

Decision making is seldom a black and white process. You need to be able to stand by and justify your convictions and realise that you won't always get a decision right.

Your values and experience will stand you in good stead making decisions. Often they will be matters where you can establish a clear picture of what is right and what is wrong. In those situations when you have certainty that what you were doing is right have strength and faith in your convictions. Back them up logically and maintain a consistent position. You make decisions with the benefit of the best information available at the time. Don't be so pig-headed that you can't realise when you have made the wrong decision. Check your progress and revisit decisions where necessary.

Leadership is doing the right thing. Management is doing things right.

Leadership and management are not the same thing. A manager needs to get a task carried out using the best method. A leader will need to successfully carry out that task using the best practices available.

Always remember that management and leadership functions are designed to complement each other. There are times when there will be disagreement on the best way forward but the goal is still the same. As a leader you are responsible for taking the direction of management and implementing it.

Anyone can say yes, a leader's job is to know when to say no.

Setting priorities and workload is necessary to ensure that the tasks that your team is committed to carry out, can be done within agreed time-lines. It is always tempting to 'over-promise', but a good leader will know the limitations of their team and how to say yes to the right things.

Agreeing to and accepting work packages and ensuring that they can be carried out is a fundamental activity for all teams. There will always be new work to pick up and these tasks will often be interesting or be regarded as high priority by customers. It's important to remember that your team's productive capacity is finite. They can only carry out a set volume of work under normal conditions and invoking alternatives such as overtime can only be maintained for a limited period before staff need to recover their work-life balance. Be realistic about taking on new work when you know the team is working at a high rate. Discuss the priorities of different work packages with customers so that you can ensure that expectations are being met and where they can't be guaranteed, you need to be open and clear about the risks that this brings. Keep your team involved in the process so that you can get the best information about what is and isn't possible. Taking on more work than your team can handle will only end up disappointing customers and creating unnecessary pressure on your team.

Being responsible sometimes means annoying people.

As the leader of a team you will be called on to make decisions that not everyone will agree with. At various times this will impact on your customers, management and staff members. Realising that this will happen before it does, helps you prepare for the difficult conversations that will follow.

Responsible leadership means juggling the expectations of different groups with different goals. Your customers will want a fast, low cost, high quality service, your management will want you to be able to provide a service that meets quality standards at a premium price in very little time, your team will want to be paid well and to do a great job without time pressure. You will have noticed that there are some mutual exclusives there. There is no magic formula to follow to make sure that everyone's expectations are met. Every situation is different and realising that you are going to have to make people accept a compromise on what they would regard as an ideal, is important so that you can manage their expectations ahead of time. They won't like it, but hopefully the service that your team provides will be valuable enough to help them accept compromises where necessary. Have this conversation with them early. Part of being a responsible leader is making sure that the groups your team interacts with (and your team) are well informed and have realistic expectations.

Respect

Respect is the practice of heeding and acknowledging the strengths and weaknesses of others and yourself in a polite way.

Leadership requires respect to be given and earned. Opportunities must be taken to demonstrate qualities that support and encourage respect. Once built it is a powerful enabler for trust and loyalty.

Respect should be examined in two ways. The first is the respect that you should show others and the second is the respect that you should earn. Take care to demonstrate that you respect those around you. Whether it's recognising good work or correcting behaviors that require improvement. People in high functioning teams will work because they believe that what they do has purpose. When you stop to think about it, this is a pretty cool thing. The way to help people *want* to carry out their work is to reinforce the *value* that they bring. The recognition is respect. If you need to correct behaviour, it should be done in a way that avoids embarrassing the individual and promotes genuine improvement. The respect you *earn* is as a result of genuine effort. The emphasis should be on the *genuine*. For example, people who work hard at jobs that don't demand a great deal of creativity or training are fully deserving of respect for their application and their determination. Whereas those who merely cruise in jobs that require considerable experience and prior learning will be less respected for their misuse of an apparent opportunity to do more. Work hard and use your skills in a genuine way to do your job and you will earn respect.

Respect and trust must be earned. Loss for either means the loss of both.

Respect and trust are separate things but deeply intertwined. Both are required qualities of a competent leader.

Being respected and trusted are characteristics that take time to develop. They are based on the observations of others and therefore they are not beliefs that *you* have, they are ones that others have *in* you. You aren't either trustworthy or respectable but others can trust or respect you. That distinction is important as it forms the core of why it's important to be able to demonstrate and sustain behaviours that will help people to put their faith in you. You have to be worthy of other's belief that you are a good person. Always remember that maintaining good relationships is about the application of consistently positive characteristics. It's difficult to have trust and respect for someone who has failed to display one or the other at some point in the past.

Obedience will not last when it's based on punishment.

People need to believe that a rule is important to follow it. If the only method of enforcing a rule is punishment when it is broken, the rule is flawed.

Ensuring that your team is able to work within reasonable bounds is achieved by setting and explaining a good set of rules. Enforcing the rules needs to be a team effort, where the reasons for following directions are clear and the consequences (immediate and long-term) are explained. Relying solely on punishment when failing to comply represents either a regulation that has no supporting argument or a dictatorial leadership system based on "*do it because I said so*". Neither can be sustained in an effective team environment.

Your superiors are as fallible as you. It's okay to question them but do it respectfully.

To imagine ourselves infallible is the height of arrogance. Therefore, do not expect your immediate superior to be infallible and when necessary ensure that you help them recognise areas for improvement.

It's a much easier job to identify and point out flaws to subordinates and yourself than to your boss. But recognising and coming forward with problems or errors is a responsibility for all levels in an organisation. Therefore you need to be comfortable pointing out where your superiors have gone wrong in a way that is not offensive and which helps them recognise the problem. To a large extent this is dependent on just how receptive your boss is to advice, but the rule of thumb should be that the better the boss they are, the easier it should be when letting them know of their mistakes. This is something that you need to keep in mind about *yourself* and your capacity to be receptive to times when *you* make a mistake. Always remember that it's a good thing when your team can tell you that something is wrong since this indicates that they have trust in your ability to receive and act on their advice appropriately. Also remember that it's better that the information come from them than that the issue manifests into something that causes a larger problem.

The respect you show your team directly affects how they feel about their work.

Your team will feel good about what they do when they are engaged in purposeful work where they receive honest, timely feedback. Your communication to them of the impact and value of their work shows respect and makes them feel better about their efforts.

Everyone wants to feel as if their efforts have been valued and have had a positive impact on the surroundings. As a leader you have a responsibility to ensure that you provide feedback on their successes and progress, both individually and as a team. This is a sign that you respect them and their work. Maintain a consistent dialogue and ensure that it is relevant and accurate. The effort that you put in reinforces the value the team provides to the wider group and good feedback about their work will help them feel good about themselves.

Respect is garnered through courtesy, not bravado.

Courtesy is a sign that you are thinking of others and that their opinion of you matters. Bravado is a sign of overconfidence that most people will see through.

Generating respect can be thought of as a continual process of demonstrating behaviour which helps others believe that you are a good person. Common courtesy is a simple and efficient mechanism that promotes positive feelings in others and helps them see you as a nice person. Attempts to impress others through making claims of abilities that could be spurious or unfounded will reinforce an impression of a person that thinks more of themselves than is justified. This will never be respected.

If a team member's behavior is unacceptable, tell them directly in private.

When dealing with unacceptable behaviour by a team member you need to ensure that you are clear about the need to change and this needs to occur in person as a private exchange.

There will be occasions when the behaviour of a team member will fall out of bounds of what is acceptable. This may be an isolated event or it may be a general trait. Either way it must be addressed in a way that ensures that the direction for change is clear and where you show your respect for the person by not embarrassing them in public. The act of dealing with the behaviour is difficult enough but by just making sure that the message is clear and by helping them retain their dignity you will make a good start to improving the situation. Having the conversation in private does not mean that it is not recorded. Quite the opposite. If the situation is serious enough to speak directly about the problem, then make sure that the person knows that you'll be drawing up a record of conversation which they will need to agree to. That doesn't mean that it is made public, but it serves as a record in the event that the behaviour is not corrected and a pattern needs to be established for more serious corrective action.

Humility

Being humble is the act of advancing a modest opinion of yourself and avoiding arrogance.

As a leader you need to be aware of your limitations and to avoid putting yourself on a pedestal. Exhibiting vanity in yourself or your abilities is a peculiar type of weakness that people are normally acutely aware of and which does not engender respect. Doing what you are required to do well and letting your actions speak for you, demonstrates your quality.

Humility is something of a double edged sword. You need to avoid arrogance and maintain a degree of modesty. This is important to help your work speak for itself and to promote respect for your efforts. But at the same time, it's important to make sure that your team and your customers know that they are being looked after by someone that takes pride in their skills and work. As in so many things, balance is important. Always err on the side of caution and lean towards humility. Take the opportunity to recognise and promote other's work and they in turn will be encouraged to complement your skills (assuming that they are genuine). Try not to go overboard and demonstrate patently false modesty. Being overly self effacing can weirdly be viewed as a deliberate attempt to draw attention to yourself and therefore be counter productive.

Admit ignorance and ask rather than blundering forward out of pride.

Appearing knowledgeable but knowing little is a false economy that ultimately fails when you are called on to deliver. Always ask for clarification.

No-one likes to appear to be ignorant. This is certainly the case in a group situation or when talking with subordinates. However, to be able to communicate effectively you need to have all the appropriate facts to hand. This means asking for clarification where it is needed. This situation is extremely common when starting a new role so lay some groundwork when you begin by letting your team know that you will be asking a lot of questions and making a point of seeking clarification of different terms and information on a pretty regular basis. Be up front about it. Take notes and look for opportunities to get as much information as possible. Also recognise that the reverse will happen when new members join your team. Go out of your way to explain some of the jargon or slang that is used in your workplace and encourage others to do the same.

Confidence without humility is arrogance.

Be aware of your strengths and limitations so that you can continue to inspire your team in a positive way.

It's important to be confident in your abilities, but no-one likes a smartass. You are in a position of leadership because you can get a group to work towards a common goal. That's not an ordinary skill. If you highlight your skills in a way that makes others feel inferior you will alienate them. Make sure that you understand that others will want you to be inspirational and clever, but they will not want you to take your skills for granted. No one will be perfect and it will require the skills and experience of a high functioning **team** to achieve different goals. Recognise that you can't lead alone. Be thankful in word and deed to those who follow you.

How we deal with defeat and victory defines us as a person.

Leadership involves accepting risk. When taking risks there will be success and failure. It's important to recognise and accept both as mechanisms for learning and improvement, not as indictments on what sort of person you are.

You will win some and you will lose some. When either occurs you need to be able to appreciate the opportunities that led you to that point in time and to use the process to develop into a better person. Winning means you need to stay humble, recognise the support structures that made it possible and look for ways to improve. Failure means putting aside the *personal* sense of failure and being objective about how to improve and succeed the next time. When you win take time to celebrate the success of the team. When you lose, make sure that the team takes something positive away from the outcome. As a person you need to be able to cope with either eventuality with grace and humility. Failure to do both marks you as short sighted and not thinking about the bigger picture.

The prestige of leadership is a distraction. Don't believe that you're better than anyone else.

Leadership has a perception of importance. Realise that you are a part of a team and as such you are as important to the efforts of the team as any other member.

If you took up a leadership position because you thought that it was a sign of having 'made it', you are mistaken. Leadership involves accepting responsibilities to help a group achieve a goal. Part of that means making decisions about how to best achieve that goal, but the kudos of success is shared by all. There is no individual prestige in leadership. There should rightfully be pride in leading a successful team and working to make that happen is simultaneously difficult and rewarding. But to imagine that your role makes you more important is to disrespect your team-mates.

Generosity

Generosity is the property of giving and sharing without an expectation of receiving anything in return.

Leadership is in large part an exercise in setting a good example with the expectation that this will have a positive effect on others. Being generous helps support those you interact with directly and it demonstrates an approach to people that encourages others to do the same.

Generosity is an investment. You can never be generous with the expectation that you will get anything in return. Always regard it as a strategic act that will only pay out indirectly. Be aware that there is a possibility of being taken advantage of in being altruistic. Don't let that stop you, but keep it in mind. Generosity is its own reward in the sense that you should feel good about yourself for doing a good thing. Also don't underestimate the positive effect on your reputation. This shouldn't be your goal, but being regarded as a good person helps form relationships which might otherwise take longer.

Share the credit and take the blame.

A leader's job is to make sure that their team is performing well and being recognised for its successes. When the team fails, its leader has failed.

If you think that leading a team will involve you being bathed in personal glory you are sadly mistaken. Teamwork is **never** about *individual* success. It's entirely appropriate to celebrate individual efforts and to recognise personal achievements, but the team needs to succeed first and foremost. A leader can only ever hope to have the opportunity to praise their team publicly and privately for a job well done. If the performance of the team has not met expectations then the leader of the team can expect to shoulder the responsibility and needs to identify how to improve.

Selflessness

Selflessness is acting in the best interests of someone else or your business instead of yourself.

Leaders are always expected to put the needs of their mission, their organization and their team above their own. They hold a position of trust that they will act altruistically in supporting their stakeholders.

The bottom line is that a leader should put their team and their organisations goals above their own needs. This is not easy but it's important to be comfortable knowing it when you take up a role. There are limits to how far this approach can be taken. It is counter-productive to run yourself into the ground and you need to ensure that you maintain a good work life balance. Ultimately your health and the well-being of your family is important to do your job well. Be upfront about your limits and your ability to maintain a high workload, but expect to go the extra mile to make things work.

Inspire and drive your team towards an agreed goal. Not to satisfy your own agenda.

Stay focussed on the the direction of your customers, management and their priorities. Remember that you work for them. Having your own ideas is great, but unless you're paying the bills, you don't get to set the goals.

As a leader of a team it is often tempting to harness the resources that you have at your disposal to carry out a pet project. Or it might be to apply your own priorities to tasks on the basis that you believe you know best how they should be scheduled. Be aware that this thinking is leading you into a dangerous area where you are commandeering a service that you are caring for, but which you do not 'own'. If you find yourself thinking that there could be a better way of doing things or that re-prioritisation could result in more efficient work, it's advisable to seek advice from up the management chain. The reality is, that if you can't make the argument for a particular action successfully to your superiors, you shouldn't be taking it.

Place your team's needs above your own.

Being selfless with your team demonstrates that you care about them and their welfare. This will encourage loyalty and commitment.

Your team is your primary tool and your responsibility. Like any complex machine it needs to be cared for and maintained to keep it operating effectively. This means realising that your responsibilities to your team have to be put first. Your team will determine their value from how you treat them. If you put your own needs first the team will assume that you do not value them as highly as when you put their needs first. When your team understand that you value them they will naturally support you and this will encourage loyalty.

Don't strive to be a success. Aim to be of value.

Being successful is an individual achievement and carries a degree of kudos. Being of value means that someone else thinks that you're doing a good job.

Trying to achieve goals and achieve success in any area is commendable and to be encouraged. However, success is not a goal in itself. It can only be relevant in a team situation when put in context with the effects of that success. The value that is generated by success or even from the effort associated with the endeavour is the greater goal.

www.ingramcontent.com/pod-product-compliance
Lightning Source LLC
Chambersburg PA
CBHW031617210526
45464CB00004B/1627